On Earth as in Heaven

The Hopes and Dreams Heart-Centered Women have for a better world, and the things they're doing to make them a reality.

Curated by: Lauren da Silva

Flourish Hub
MEDIA CO.

Flourish Hub Media Company

"When I was a boy and I would see scary things in the news, my mother would say to me, 'Look for the helpers. You will always find people who are helping."
Fred Rogers

Contents

Introduction

Lauren da Silva

One of the best things about my life over the past few years has been that I have been privileged to sit at the feet of women from all walks of life, and from all corners of the globe as they share, unpack, and flesh out the dreams they have for the worlds that they live in... and I have had a front row seat as they took their first few steps into making their dreams a reality.

I have often closed out a coaching call, shut down my laptop and taken a deep breath as I wondered out loud to myself, "why don't we share *these* stories more?"

We live in a world that glamorizes overnight successes, grand gestures, fortune and fame. We put these people on pedestals and hold them up against out ordinary, boring and uneventful lives as the standard we should all aspire to.

And yet, all around us... on our streets, in our churches, in our grocery stores and in our school pick up lines are men and women who are taking one step at a time towards a life and building world that is more beautiful than many of us could ever imagine.

This book is a collection of the dreams I have been privy to, and a window into my own dreams. I have often day-dreamed about collecting all of the dreams, visions and goals the women I know are working towards and compiling them in one place. Whenever the world felt dark and hopeless, I would read it from cover to cover and be reminded that there are helpers, and more importantly, that there is light shining all around us... if only we had eyes to see it, and faith to believe in and nurture it.

This book is my own dream come true.

Some of these stories are written as bold manifestos, some as stories, and others take us on a backstage tour of their dreamer's visions.

My hope is that as you read them, that you will immerse yourself not just in the world that these women are slowly but surely shaping into existence with their everyday lives, but that they would also rekindle or ignite your own dreams for a better world. And that they would inspire you to take one step to making your own dreams a reality.

·····•·•····

As the daydream of collecting these stories started to take shape, I found myself enamoured by campfire experiences. I am a grown woman with three young children, so for at least the past decade, campfires have always meant making sure someone doesn't get too close, incinerate their appendages or their s'mores, or get sticky, melted chocolate all over me and my winter woolies.

Over the past few years, particularly since weathering the worst of the COVID-19 pandemic and social isolation, I have huddled around campfires with other grown women, visiting late into dark winter, fall, and early spring nights, just sharing our lives and stories.

There is something about the warm, inviting glow crackling away amid cold, dark silence that creates a moment in time as the darkness isolates us from the rest of the world and our real lives, and we feel safe at that moment to lay our soul-selves bare before one another.

I wanted this book to feel like one of those cold fall nights around a campfire with my friends.

So dearest reader, I invite you to imagine yourself pulling up a blanket, a camping chair, a log, or an old lawn chair to the fire. Imagine that we are alone in the darkness, our hearts and faces glowing in the warmth at the center of our circle. This book is what happens when you invite women just like you to share the bravest moments of their lives and when you hold space for them to do so.

Something else that I think is important for you to know is that there are women from at least five continents and countless more cultures, languages, and walks of life represented in this book. We have done our best to preserve what we've endearingly called their "writing accents" in their storytelling. For this reason, contributions switch periodically between British and American English writing standards. Very few of them are professional writers and authors, but all are brave and doing the work of being and becoming who they truly are. We hope that you enjoy the diversity represented around the fire, and that you'll notice how universal our humanity is.

1

You are Worthy of Your Dreams

As It Was Meant to Be
Christianna Johnson
Gautier, Mississippi. United States.

Have you ever hated the sight of someone or couldn't stand their voice? You had a critique for everything they did or said. If you never saw them again, life would be great. I felt that way about myself.

From my teenage years to my early twenties, I hated myself. I disconnected from myself so much that I didn't know what *I* wanted in life. I knew what other people wanted for theirs, so I'd try on *their* ideas, but nothing fit.

I didn't think I was allowed to want things, and I didn't believe I was capable of wanting good or worthy things. One way this developed was through my upbringing. My parents did their best, but I've come to realize they were emotionally immature and distant in a lot of ways. I thought I'd receive more praise, attention, and affirmation if I were a 'good' child. There were many stresses and demands on them, but I didn't understand that back then. I only knew that I didn't get what I wanted, and it felt terrible. So I concluded that I was bad, and that was why they wouldn't give me what I needed.

Instead of seeking attention, I withdrew from people and myself and made my needs small. I stopped wanting and dreaming. That was too risky and scary. It was better to live life wedged into a corner than out where people could see me.

One of the many problems with that plan was that I still had myself. The self I did not like.

To cope with my self-loathing, I numbed my feelings so that I couldn't name them. I blocked sadness and anger, but I couldn't pick which other emotions got blocked. I also blocked joy and happiness, curiosity and wonder. I couldn't process my feelings or emotions – I didn't know how and didn't know anyone who could help me. I didn't understand what I was doing to myself.

Then I discovered storytelling.

I didn't have to be with myself when I visited a story. I was with the characters and exploring their worlds. My mom had a tote box full of books. After finishing them, I read through most of my local library. I wondered if I could write stories myself. Then I started college to become a medical laboratory scientist. At the same time, I wrote fantasy stories about magical people in impossible places.

I'd found something that I loved — telling stories, and it came from me. I shared them online in forums with other readers and writers, and they liked my stories too. For the first time, I realized I could make something good that I loved and that others valued, too. I wrote over fifty stories, more than 200,000 words in three years. I didn't tell anyone in real life that I wrote. I *knew* they would say it was a waste of time because my stories weren't about God or real life. The heroes won against the bad guys, the people who were supposed to fall in love with each other did, and impossible victories happened.

Good always won in the end.

I had something to focus on besides how much I didn't like myself, how stressful college was, how much I missed my siblings now that they'd moved out, or how lonely I was. I was able to experience emotions through stories – even if one character was blue and the other could read minds. When I wrote stories people enjoyed and connected with, I felt like *I* connected with those people too. It grounded me back into my body, and I could *feel* again. My stories were one good thing about me; they also made others happy. It was like magic.

I was a good writer and storyteller.

But as I entered my final semester of college, I had an internship and needed to study to pass. So, I stopped writing. Then I graduated and started in the workforce.

I didn't write again for over three years, and I lost my connection with that magic feeling.

That was almost a decade ago. Since then, I've grown and learned to love myself, and I speak that love over myself. I've forgiven myself and others for the past, healed, and continued the process.

One of my tools is journaling. I started that after I made a few good friends. As I interacted with them, I realized I needed to speak to them differently than I did to myself, at least if I wanted them to *stay* my friends. Sarcasm is defined as 'to cut the flesh,' and I was a butcher.

I became aware of my negative self-talk through journaling and re-programmed how I spoke to myself. It was scary to see how I thought and how dark my mindset was. I made a conscious effort to catch those thoughts. It was hard to do, and it felt weird to be gentle. I'd speak to myself as if I were a child, picturing my little niece in my mind.

As I journaled, I learned about myself and how to connect with my feelings and dreams again. Unknowingly, I was practicing neuroplasticity, but I knew Scripture said to think about good and lovely things. Journaling brought me back around to storytelling, and I became less critical about the idea of doing something commercial with my writing. After all that time, I still had the pull.

Could I make a living as a writer?

I spent years studying writing craft, stopped, and started. I was published in two anthologies, but no books on my own. Journaling and building a community with my friends had improved my mindset, but I still needed more. I knew it was possible to be a self-published author. I consumed all the podcasts, books, and videos I could find. But I couldn't make it happen for myself.

It wasn't until my sister persuaded me to buy a home-based business program that I realized my dreams didn't have to stay dreams, and I could live them out in reality.

What was my dream?

Storytelling. Connecting with people through words. Giving them reasons to stay a while longer. Self-publishing and freelancing as a writer.

My dream was not only to write but to create a media company. I wanted to build a thriving, seven-figure media company based in Mississippi that would be known across the country. A company that would employ dozens of people and feed families. A company that would give millions of dollars away to worthy causes and make an impact. A company that would leave an inheritance and a legacy for my family's generations.

I dreamed of creating freedom.

I am worthy of my calling.

This thought has evolved as my mindset has expanded. I am worthy as I am, and I always have been. A pastor said that God created us in His image and then re-creates us throughout our lives to become more like Him. Nothing can come from God that isn't like Him.

If God is worthy and we come from Him, we bear His image. Since He doesn't create anything unlike Him, then we are worthy.

If I am worthy, that means my gifts and dreams are worthy. My dreams are meant to be reality because the One who made me gave them to me. We have our dreams for a reason. Everything in our lives is for a reason – nothing is wasted. Not even when we find ourselves trapped in our boring, corporate jobs as we try to build the dream.

At the end of 2021, I let my career go. I'm so sad that my sister-in-law's sudden death and the arrival of her children in my home prompted that decision. She and I were both twenty-eight years old, and my niece and nephew were eight and four months old. But nothing is a waste, not one moment of pain, not a single tear, even though that can seem cruel.

When it's close enough or if we're empathic enough, death makes us consider death. But death can also inspire us to live. When I thought of myself dead at twenty-eight, I had to ask myself about that.

Did I live authentically?

Did I love well?

Had I honored the dreams and gifts I was given?

Did I live a life that made me joyful and inspired others to live full of joy?

Would heaven look anything like what I'd created here?

Or had I just been living out a lesser kind of hell?

In *The Great Divorce*, C. S. Lewis describes hell, not as a place of fire and burning and brimstone. He illustrates a nothing town full of dull people who live days that all look the same as the one before. They're eternally searching for something they can never find. There is no color, no beauty, and no true life.

Some of us relate more to that kind of hell: a hell of sameness. We never get the thing we want. It's not for us, right? We're just not one of the lucky ones.

That's a scarcity story.

Jackie Hill Perry is an author, speaker, and poet. She shared about King David of the Bible on Instagram, saying, "David was trained to defeat enemies through effective means and was a man of war for decades. So it shouldn't surprise us that he utilized those same techniques when murdering Uriah. When sin has your heart, *it'll use your gifts too*."

David's story made me think of my story. I'm not a warrior, king, or murderer. But one story sparks another.

Sin means to miss the mark, like an arrow that didn't strike true. For years, I told myself this story about not being good, worthy, or driven enough to pursue my dreams. I missed the mark and used my gifts to make myself crazy, turning my life's story into a tragedy.

We are all books or epistles, being written by our Creator, God, who has outlined the story of our lives. He holds the pen but lets us co-author. We co-create our lives. We see the stories of those around us and before us, and they help shape our story while we contribute to theirs.

The stories we tell now and pass to our children will shape the world moving forward. Isn't that how we all came to be here, at this moment? Someone *before* co-created our *now*.

I'm so grateful my story didn't end at twenty-eight or earlier. I have so much more to share.

I'm building a legacy. I'm not a mom or wife and may never be. But I still have children; my niece and nephew. I will show them what it looks like to have freedom and joy. I will show them that the desires inside them are good, and they are responsible for aligning those desires with good to become all they are meant to be.

My niece and nephew are young now, but they get to see my growth through the process. Maybe they'll want to know how I did it and get involved when they're older. Perhaps they'll want something different, and I'll be able to help them go after the dreams in their heart so they can create the life they choose.

They'll understand what it means to make a heaven of earth then. Even though I'm in the middle of my journey, I'm not waiting for the future to be happy and joyful now. Holding the vision and walking forward can be challenging, but I'm committed to seeing the dream come alive.

It all begins with our words, our thoughts, our beliefs, and our choices.

I've created a place for writers and authors, a community on Facebook. I'm building something in there.

This community is full of education and accountability for introverted women who want to create a career out of their words. It's for women who love stories and creating and want connection and knowledge. I believe my path is laid out and that I co-create this life with my Creator. He gave me my gifts for a purpose. If your path and gifts align with mine, let's go together. I invite you to come with me. Whether this is a first meeting or a last, know this:

You are now and have always been worthy.

ABOUT THE AUTHOR:
Christianna Johnson

B orn and raised in Mississippi, Christianna Johnson has been in love with words and stories since she learned to read at four years old. While she worked a responsible 9 - 5 job for years, she built her skills and knowledge in writing, self-publishing, and business. As an introvert, she has always enjoyed reading and quiet adventures with dynamic characters and actionable wisdom from experts.

After becoming a full-time writer in 2021, she has created a community for others like her — The Introverted Writers Club is a space where other writers can learn, grow, and connect with each other.

Connect with Christianna:

2

The Desert Draws You Nearest to the Oasis

Renee Emus
Waco, Texas. United States.

Lush, fruitful land provided an abundance to meet all our needs. Perfect relationships with our Creator existed here. This was the Garden. When sin entered, this world became one that we were not intended to live in.

Today, I may feel distant from God, but He has never left me. I yearn for Garden experiences, perfect relationships, and abundant provision. He is still here, patiently waiting for me to open the door. God is not one to force entry or bust it down, but always knocks ever so gently as a sweet reminder of His presence.

"God, where are you?" *I am here.* "I don't see you." *Look.* "I don't feel you."

Selah.

Newly married and filled with optimism about our relationship, my husband and I moved to his hometown in Kenya in 2019. We were warned of the rough waters that can ebb and flow in a marriage. Some said, "It'll be tough," or "Marriage can be difficult at times," but you really don't know what that means until you experience it for yourself. It is only when you encounter your own desperate need for grace and receive it that you can offer it to others. I was confident that we could handle anything that came our way with the Holy Spirit as our guide. My husband's ministry goal was to assist families in becoming self-sufficient through horticulture practices and growing their own food, a foreign concept to traditionally semi-nomadic people, raising animals as their only source of food. I hoped to learn much from this new community I now called home. My priorities were to learn the language and the culture through immersion and support my husband with his gardens while I made plans to work with the Deaf people in the community. Working in ministry is tough to navigate. My husband and I were working together more and seeing completely new sides of each other. Working in ministry within a deeply corrupted organization, as newlyweds, in a foreign land that I struggled to navigate, brought a whole new meaning to "tough."

Prior to our arrival in Kenya, the U.S. board of the organization we were working with discovered sexual abuse of minors among the local Kenyan leadership. Unfortunately, this is a common story that is played out in greater Kenya. This type of abuse had become so common that abuse was the norm, not the exception. The weight of hearing these children's stories while adapting to my new home was an unbearable load to carry. We never knew who we could trust. Relationships were marred from the beginning due to our association with this organization. People with power had eyes all over town, and I lived in fear of being kidnapped and forced to 'inform' on our friends.

In my daily life, the smell of charcoal reminded me that I could not start the jiko (the stove) myself. My knuckles were rubbed raw and blistered from washing our clothes by hand, which forced me to confront the privileged life I had led. I couldn't communicate directly with my grandmother-in-law or many of the people in our community, and I sorely felt the lack of genuine, deep relationships.

One week, we went to a city-wide carnival full of rides, food, and shop vendors. Some boys living on the street were following our group and making obscene comments about me to each other based on my skin color and my being a woman. One of our students couldn't stand to hear what they were saying and asked them to move on and stop following us. They refused and slashed our student's back with a razor blade multiple times.

A few days later, I was at the market with my friend while she bought a new phone. I had to leave early, so I couldn't stay with her until she had completed her errands. She later told me the salesman wanted to charge her double for the phone she wanted because she was "friends with a white lady." When she refused to pay the exorbitant price, he slapped her across the face. My husband returned to the shop with her and got a fair price.

To this day, my grandmother-in-law is refused government benefits that the elderly receive for food and other expenses because her grandson is married to a white lady.

When the color of my skin causes harm to those I love, having true, genuine relationships with people becomes impossible. These situations reminded me that I will always be perceived as wealthy, whether true or not.

Being from this town, my husband was supposed to guide me through the language barrier and help me learn the cultural nuances so some of these heartaches could have been avoided altogether. Instead of teaching me how to swim, he seemed to believe that 'throwing me in the deep end' was better, and I was drowning.

While we pressed on for the children's sake, our marriage silently suffered. Typical newlywed disagreements were compounded by the weight of culture shock and the turmoil of working within a broken organization. The stress and trauma built as we were forced to flee our home, navigating a flooded river that turned a day's journey into three.

We were headed to a new town and a new organization that we thought was safe. Once settled, my husband and I decided to apply to participate in a discipleship class in Uganda recommended by dear friends of ours. Our applications were accepted, and we headed to Uganda by bus after the New Year. Months later, it was discovered that the leadership in this new organization the children were seeking refuge in was communicating with the very abusers we had fled from. The chaos of a broken world continued.

My husband and I were very hopeful about the class in Uganda. It typically had students from various Western and African countries and teachers from Uganda, America, and England. The purpose of the class was to discuss our worldviews, debunk our respective cultures' myths, then dive deep into the Bible to discover the truth. This class was a perfect fit for us; for our ministry goals and as a biracial-bicultural couple.

Just as I began to see a glimmer of hope for our future, we sank even lower. The interesting thing about hidden sin and secrets is that they will always come to light in due time, whether you want them to or not.

In Uganda, I discovered that my husband had other children with some women in Kenya and that he depended on smoking as a stress reliever. How? How did I not see this? How could he have married me without telling me? How could I have been so stupid, so blind? I felt bamboozled.

This began a grieving process that then led me to the emotions of hurt, anger, and mourning for the dreams and expectations I had for our marriage and my life. I did not have my familiar community from the West, but God provided a community for me in Uganda that allowed me to process the hurt and culturally navigate the 'why.'

As I was processing, I felt an obligation to tell those that stood by us in support at our wedding. These people, and all in attendance, have a responsibility, to an extent, to keep my husband and me accountable to our vows. I was not ready to hear their input, advice, or opinions – I just needed to give them an update and hopefully process as I was telling them.

Some people insisted they remind me that the Bible allows for divorce in instances like ours. Others believed that I was not able to see clearly or think rationally and needed to make decisions for my own sake. Not only was I separated from my support network by a physical distance, but their unwarranted opinions about my situation also began to separate us relationally.

I had lost the husband I thought I had married, the trust of dear friends and some family, and I felt completely alone. Who would support me? Who could I turn to for help? Who could comfort me?

"Knock, knock, remember I am here." God would arrive with gentle reminders. Through imagery, through His Word, and through worship, I was able to hear His voice. I learnt to drop the walls meant to protect me and melt in His presence, fully and unashamedly me. God revealed that my marriage seemed broken, but He had big plans for our future family and for us. *"Trust in me for what you cannot yet see."* This revelation was hard to explain and even harder to believe, especially to those I had just informed of my husband's deceit.

Throughout this entire experience, I dreamt of the Garden of Eden: the perfect garden and perfect relationships, a land of no abuse, a land of understanding. Oh, how I yearned for this. Oddly enough, I was experiencing a glimpse of this Garden.

I am reminded of the Israelites' wanderings, how they were set free from their physical bondage, yet they continued moaning about returning to the familiar while failing to understand the lesson that God was teaching them. I, too, was groaning to return to my comfortable, familiar bondage in the West, and I was failing to see what God was teaching me. When in the West, I idolized my community by running to them for advice before running to God. Now, I was stripped of that comfort and confronted with my own sin, which allowed God to show me how sweet a relationship with Him is. I was incredibly uncomfortable and lonely. I was scared, but God always provides. He provided for the Israelites through daily manna (sustenance). Although manna was not desirable, when compared to the alternative (starvation), manna tasted sweet. The Lord provided me with a relationship with Him that I know I would not have gained in my comfortable Western bondage.

My desert experience in East Africa was necessary for me to have the relationship I currently have with my Lord. Going through my desert of pain, isolation, and betrayal shifted my perspective and caused me to be completely dependent on the Lord's provisions in my own life. Ironically, the desert gave me the clearest glimpse of the Garden. The pain and suffering I was experiencing made me hyper-aware of the goodness that God originally intended for me at creation. When we are surrounded by darkness, we are most able to appreciate the gentle shimmer of the stars. I have learned to look beyond the barren land and look up to see the beauty. Today, I am *thankful* for my time in the desert. My relationship with God was strengthened and deepened through this trek, and as I face daily trials, I rely on lessons learned during that time.

Even though I live in a broken world, I must actively seek these Heaven on Earth moments. If this looks like wandering in the desert for a time, Lord, give me strength and endurance. I ask God to give me his eyes so I can see his creations, His people, as He sees them. I depend on His grace daily so that I may extend this grace to others. Living in Kenya, it would have been easy for me to reject all God was teaching me, give up, and return to the familiar comforts of the West. Instead, I would often ask God to show me his plans. Rather than showing me His map, He would only reveal the next right step for me to take.

As I partner with my Creator, I see glimpses of what he intended Earth to be like. I see this through nature, people, and living things. I experience this through moments of peace, loving relationships, and unity – none of which come easily. I surrender my hands and feet and ask God to co-create a glimpse of the Garden for me and those around me.

Many days, I lose focus and stray as if I were a carthorse without blinders. Sometimes I stray a few paces off course before I hear my Creator's gentle call. *"I am here."* Other times I wander entirely out of the arena, far away from Him.

When we find ourselves in the desert, our human tendency is to see the dry, barren land with no water in sight. Oh, how easily we fixate on the physical things right in front of us! How quickly we forget our constant companion who desires to lead us to the water and provide for us if we let him! Take courage and look up. Ask God to help you see as he sees and for a generous portion of His grace so that you may extend it generously to those around you. Pray for strength and endurance for the journey ahead because although the desert is vast, it is the unexpected pathway to the Garden. And you were created for the Garden.

ABOUT THE AUTHOR:
Rene Emus

R enee Emus is a wife and mother of two kids; one will be born in October 2022. She is a teacher for the Deaf and hard of hearing and is passionate about the Deaf community worldwide knowing Jesus' name. She graduated from Baylor in 2016 with a degree in Deaf Education. Renee has lived in Kenya and had plans to get to know the Deaf there before COVID hit, but now she is using her skillset to teach Deaf and hard-of-hearing kids in Waco, Texas.

Connect with Rene:

3

A World Where Women's Bodies Experience Life & Vitality

The Chasm
Chelsea Macias
Austin, Texas. United States.

There's a gaping chasm in the world we live in that, as a registered dietitian, I have a mission to help fill. This is the void between our bodies and the joy of living a full life inside them. I believe there are two types of people in this chasm. Those who watch life go by and those who choose to live fully in its uncomfortable and uncontrollable chaos. In essence, neither disposition is good nor bad. Each is simply a way of being in this world. Sometimes, I'd rather be the person who sits and watches life go by, but that's not the way God made me.

God made me with 'just' a dash of emotion. I have *so much* emotion and empathy that as much as I try to wrangle it, there is no submission. I spent years fighting my overwhelming compassionate response to friends in challenging situations. I spent so many nights wishing I was not as vulnerable as I am or that I was less emotional. Those were futile efforts because wishing could never change the essence of who God made me – an empath to my core.

A wise counselor once told me, "empathy, when left without coping skills, leads to anxiety." As I got older, letting emotions rule me became the pattern of my coping skills. The only skills I had were to let my feelings rule me for weeks until I resorted to numbing myself with alcohol. I would become anxious and then depressed. I would sit on the floor sobbing for no reason. During a particularly rough season dealing with postpartum anxiety, I walked into a psychologist's office that would change my life.

She changed my life through the simple act of teaching me mindfulness. She sat with me as I sat with my emotions. They felt like a freight train slamming into me physically and emotionally. It was tormenting to reveal the shameful anxious thoughts that were occurring, and it was scary watching my brain work from the outside. However, the breakthrough came when I was able to bring my anxious brain into the light. Ultimately, the emotions subsided, and I was led to curiosity. Where did this come from? Why was I thinking this way? Was it actually true?

Eventually, the freight train passed, and I learned to hear my inner compassionate spirit. I began talking to myself like a friend. I talked myself down off the anxious cliff daily. Years later, there are some days I don't have anxious thoughts anymore. I still have anxiety patterns where I get amped up or fixated on something. However, through my mindfulness work, I have cultivated that inner compassionate friend that can help me when needed.

To cultivate the joy of living a full life, I found it was vital for me to hear my inner compassionate friend. Some people find their inner friend through religion or spirituality. Others find yoga or weight lifting is a productive outlet for their emotions.

The trick is to deal with negative thoughts as they happen, not after. Acknowledging and leveraging our emotions helps us learn to flourish wholly and completely.

THE POWER

I believe my empathy is a gift from God. It's a superpower and part of what He used to make me a counselor. At 14, I remember asking myself how I would have a career that made a difference in this world. I swear God chuckled because He knew what He had in store, and he knew that my body would be the centerpiece of fully embracing who He made me to be.

It started at first with knee pain coming around the age of 14. The doctor dismissed it, and it eventually went away, only to return as I moved into my first apartment at 18. Then later, I experienced debilitating knee, shoulder, and hip pain from something as simple as sleeping on the wrong bed. The doctor dismissed it because all the tests and scans were negative for anything remarkable.

"Just take some pain relievers," was all the doctors said. But I knew there was something deeper going on.

Still suffering with these mysterious joint issues, I became pregnant at 21, and overnight, my joint pain disappeared. But it came roaring back during the postpartum period. I went down the research rabbit hole. I found supplements that would decrease my pain level dramatically, and after a round of the Whole 30 diet, I was able to move freely without pain for the first time in years.

This was incredible news! No pain relievers involved? This transformation meant my body wasn't going to be crumbling by the age of 30. I could jump, run, swing, scooter, and climb all I wanted to because my body was able.

That experience ignited a passion within me. I wanted to seek the restoration of people to food. It fueled me to seek out the healing power within food. The process led me to encounter God's creation at its core. Through my studies, I was able to serve and support those who were wealthy, impoverished, broken, or healthy—those in their most vulnerable states. The joy and the pain were stunning.

It's been a privilege to guide the scared pregnant mother on WIC trying to navigate life with an unexpected pregnancy. It's been a privilege to help a soldier trying to figure out what he needs to prepare for starvation during special forces training. It has also been an honor to walk with friends and family through the depths of wicked autoimmune diseases. The empath in me thrives as I connect and offer healing guidance to those in the depths of their pain.

When our society fails to support someone struggling with their health, God uses me through my past struggles and victories to cover them with his overwhelming grace.

THE RESTORATION

We are taught by culture that one standard is acceptable, but this standard is impossible to live up to. For example, a certain body fat percentage, curves like Marilyn Monroe, a thigh gap, or six-pack abs have all been idealized. Our culture has worshiped these 'ideal' bodies over the last 100 years. More recently, I have seen women tearing themselves apart in the comparison game fueled by photo filters, photoshop, and those whose only job is to make their bodies look a certain way.

It's important to remind these struggling women that God LOVES our earthly bodies. Not in a vain way, but in how each individual is just that – individual. Our bodies are inherently beautiful because He made them! He gave us this wonderful thing called DNA. It's designed so intricately that siblings have the same parents and gene pool to come from, but they are never the same.

The fear and self-loathing of women in our culture come out early in conversations. They are scared for the future of their health, and their fear has been propagated by unbelief in their own bodies. It has been fueled by years of neglect and criticism by themselves and others. They resort to coping with hate and let that fuel destructive dieting cycles. They are simply seeking physical changes to their body. Ultimately these diets result in temporary success, failure to achieve the long-term results, and self-esteem that's in the toilet.

In my work, we get to unwind all those negative opinions and cultural biases against ourselves. This means sitting with people as they recount the experiences that led them into the full-blown depths of anorexia. It can take the form of recounting the fears and medical trauma. It can mean divulging the deep secrets that led to a mistrust of their body and its ability to work for them. As people move through this process, it shines a light into the dark places of relational issues with food and the body. That's where they learn to love themselves and appreciate what their body has done for them! Everyone needs to rewire their relationship with food and their body. The Bible says, "where there is light, there can be no darkness." When the light is shining brightly, although it may hurt for a little while, the evil of this world no longer has a place in that relationship.

THE CALL

There's a story in the Bible in the book of John. Jesus asks the apostle Peter, "Peter do you love me?" Peter replies, "Yes, Lord!" Jesus then commands him to "Feed my sheep." Jesus commands Peter to do this three times! If there's anything I've learned from scripture, it's that if Jesus says something three times, you'd better listen up.

I take this command so literally in my life, and I ask God daily to help me live out that story. Now, it's not feeding people, but guiding the sheep to the pasture with nourishing foods and letting them choose where they want to graze. The beautiful thing is that everyone eats and everyone has a relationship with food. That is the place God calls dietitians to serve.

My mission is to foster the restoration of people to their bodies. Only God can do that fully! It may never be complete while living, but we can work hard to nourish and thrive the earthly temple in which the holy spirit resides.

I frequently say, "You can do anything with one person in your corner at all times."

That is me. I try hard to be that person with love, compassion, tough words, and problem-solving skills when needed.

I feel as if I am only one person sounding the gong of great joy that can be heard in this earthly temple. What I want you to know, what I want my people to know, is that restoration is possible. It may never be complete. That's for God to do in heaven. BOY, am I thankful that I don't have to be the completer of all good works. But it is possible to have a support system that helps you thrive physically, spiritually, and emotionally. You can conquer and continue to try new things that may help your ailing body or soul.

Not everyone is ready or will ever be ready to heal their relationship with food or their body, or to experience God in that way. That is something I have to be ok with. For some, restoration and sanctification may come in other ways that don't involve connecting back to their body and truly loving it for everything that it does. Those people will still stand next to me in heaven, fully healed, living in glorious eternity. In the meantime, I labor here on earth. I work for the restoration of men and women to have healthy, happy, and whole bodies. This restoration helps them live out the mission God has called them to here on this earth.

Selah.

ABOUT THE AUTHOR
Chelsea Macias

C helsea Macias, RDN is a native of San Antonio, Texas. She is a third generation registered dietitian that built her business, The Food Sensitivity Institute, on the intersection of her passion for people, culinary arts, and the intricacies of the human body. Chelsea's husband is currently serving our country in the Texas Army National Guard and they resided in Austin, Texas with their two children and dog, Banjo.

Connect with Chelsea:

4

A World Where All Feel Permission to Experience Joy

An Invitation to Joy
Jessica Blankenship
New Richmond, Ohio. United States.

I t took me a long time to realize that just because I interpreted something a certain way didn't mean it actually happened that way.

Somewhere along the line, I got the message that being creative, being an artist, and especially being an art teacher was a ridiculous idea. It was frivolous, embarrassing, and irresponsible somehow.

Did anyone ever say these things to me? I don't recall.

Did I get that message from my church leaders? No way.

Did my parents and teachers mean to inflict this emotional chokehold on me? Absolutely not.

Not even close. Actually, it wasn't a message to me at all. It was a perspective, a vibe of foreboding joy, passed on to me unknowingly—a perspective of "equating difficulty with virtue and art with fooling around," according to Julia Cameron.

I'll add this – art and joy are often synonymous with one another.

It wasn't "art" that was frowned upon, it was JOY. It was the fear of being unprepared for a disaster; it was "fooling around." It was the mindset that misery equaled being responsible, focused, sensible, and grown-up, as if anxiousness meant being focused on reality.

Jesus warned us not to worry or to be anxious.

He asked us to consider the lilies and the birds of the air, and to take no thought for tomorrow ... for each day has sufficient trouble of its own.

But he also said to trim your lamps, to be ready, and keep watch.

Scripture reminds us to be attentive.

If you are wired like I am, this was a constant lesson that fear,
and worry,
and over-thinking,
and stressing out
are the opposites of faith.

I justified my anxiety and stress by claiming that I was concerned and prepared, as a mature Christian was supposed to be. I've 'dress rehearsed' all the potential bad things that could happen and lost sleep because I am so 'responsible.'

If I'm honest, it really came down to fear – fear of being caught off guard, embracing vulnerability, and looking foolish when the other shoe dropped. It was fear of looking frivolous and fear of getting overtaken in joy.

Does someone have to be convinced that JOY is a good thing to feel?

I had to be convinced. I was called out; PRAYED over. It took four preachers separately, unbeknownst to one another, to call me up at four different churches. I definitely wasn't going to stand up and request prayer for myself – to feel JOY. Really? Isn't that the most FRIVOLOUS prayer??

28

My mind was a whirlwind. I cannot articulate the feelings I felt at those services. Did the God of Heaven and Earth really care that I was living in torment in my mind? I was a slave to anxiety about every little thing in every moment. I wanted to be taken seriously, and I was frustrated with myself. I hated the quiet, bitter person I had become – a person afraid to feel joy.

I was afraid to be who God made me, to be vulnerable, and embrace my calling. I was afraid of trying and failing daily at gaining credibility and validity. I was afraid of being seen as frivolous, silly, and irresponsible. I was afraid of feeling – and specifically feeling JOY, even though I didn't know it yet.

I remember being in a church service when it felt like the preacher was preaching about everything I was going through. I was sheepishly looking around, wondering if anyone else was experiencing the same thing. The first message was about being enslaved. Everything the singer and preacher said cut deep. I wanted to embrace the message. I wanted to feel, but I felt so tightly chained up that I sat in the back row, nodding passively. At the end of the service, there was an altar call, and several people went up. I convinced myself that I was insane because I had nothing to identify as the cause of my torment. My adult life had zero obvious struggles. How could this message be for me?

Finally, the preacher looked at me and pointed directly at me in the back row, in front of the whole church. He said, "Sister Jessica, it's you." I felt a wave of relief because I wanted so badly for it to be for me. I needed someone to call me out and give me permission to take hold of that sermon and apply it to my heart. I needed an invitation. I needed that man to obey God so that I felt worthy of people surrounding me in prayer, praying for my heart to be unshackled from fear and anxiety – to embrace JOY and victory in Christ.

Even typing this, I feel worried that someone will read this and roll their eyes at me again; but I know that others out there need a path marked out for them.

That night, I cried out to God about this invisible but heavy weight on my shoulders. People encircled me, not knowing what they were praying for. Another sister led me around the church as we lifted our hands and prayed together. The preacher kept saying, "Look not to the left nor to the right." He knew that I was worried about people looking at me.

The other three services happened similarly. Why did God have to send others to get my attention? Because when I went home each time, I still lived like I was in bondage with fear, shame, and over-thinking that was debilitating. I needed to intentionally WALK IN VICTORY, so I didn't become entangled again.

Then, I had a dear friend clarify it all. I was telling her that I felt confused about my business, calling, and ministry. I had tried so many things that hadn't felt right for me. Every attempt was like pushing a boulder uphill, and it was heavy. I had been on several paths trying to be seen and labeled as responsible and worthwhile.

I had created an online Christian marriage course for struggling marriages but wasn't confident enough to release it into the world and ended up deleting it completely.

I had become Dave Ramsey fluent and was very close to deciding to become a certified financial coach.

I had become obsessed with natural health and felt it necessary to teach people what I'd learned.

I had earned a master's degree in gifted education even though I knew I never wanted to teach the material.

I had tried teaching art to adults, thinking that 'real artists' surely can't teach children.

Finally, I experienced a change in my teaching position in my district because of the pandemic when art, music, and physical education were restructured. After being moved out of art, my new teaching position was a fourth-grade homeroom.

As an art teacher who wasn't getting to teach art during that time, I felt another wave of that old feeling – that art was frivolous, unimportant, and silly. "You, Jessica, are frivolous, unimportant, and silly. No one takes you seriously."

That conversation with a friend helped me. I explained that I was feeling a pull into teaching art again and starting a business to do that on a larger scale and that it felt so incredibly worthless, and I was scared to tell anyone.

After listening and giving me some guidance, she asked me this. "All these art dreams sound amazing, and it sounds like you are afraid of that. Have you given yourself PERMISSION to feel JOY?"

Tears. Lots of them. God had sent four preachers to me earlier to tell me I was entering a season of joy. But I was ingrained in a lifestyle of misery and foreboding joy and didn't know it. It was so foggy that I couldn't see my own way.

Permission. I hadn't allowed the God of the universe to penetrate my heart and transform me out of the 'realistic' person I was. The last church service was the one that brought lasting victory to my anxious heart. The preacher said to me, "You have to let God take it from you." Let God! That night, that's exactly what I did. Hands raised. Tears of surrender. A voice of wailing from within me. I gave it up to God.

That night, I allowed God to take away the torment in my mind. I know this sounds dramatic. But it was life-changing. A door of Heaven was opening above me and reminding me that I am not supposed to fear. I am not supposed to live with weights on my mind. Jesus came that we might have life and that more abundantly.

Could something fun and joyful like teaching art and inspiring families be worthwhile, valid, and meaningful? Is it possible that God was talking about abundance in this way when Jesus said he came to bring abundant life? Could this be part of God's will on Earth, as it is in Heaven?

Making art with kids is fun. Teaching art to children is fun. It is awakening a bit of wonder in their minds that they didn't see before and it shows on their faces.

It is stirring a joyous search in them.

Can I participate in this joy? Is this my calling – to cast a vision for joy and wonder for children and adults in this messed-up world?

Through artists' eyes, wonder is a return to an old-fashioned concept. I don't think of grand ideas when I think of wonder and awe. Instead, I think of simple things, calm things, beautiful things, and a slowness that is lacking in modern life. I think of simple things that would elude us if we were not being mindful. In education, we often seek more amazing things to engage students who are chronically hooked on technology and often lack healthy social interactions.

It's simply 'wonder inflation.' We cannot teach kids to depend on grandiose adventures. Instead, we must model how we can find wonder in small things and that we're not in competition with entertainment.

I believe and know that we can capture their attention and interest and even harness some mindfulness in these young minds if we can model *wonder*. We must show them the opportunities for wonder and cultivate an atmosphere of wonder. We must teach them to pause.

My grandpa did this often. He would inspect things. He noticed things. He wasn't in a hurry. He was aware and interested in people and thoughtful.

In our full-speed survival mode, we have inadvertently taught kids not to invest time, energy, and wonder.

Perhaps we have set these low expectations by not planning projects that are more lengthy, layered, and multi-stepped.

Maybe this is my gift and my calling. Now that the air is clear in my mind and my heart is free from inner turmoil, I see that my gifts are unique, and I am dreaming again!

I have goals of writing and illustrating children's books to create something that is a cross between my love of illustrations and my love of literature. There is innocence in art and communication in images. I love scripture, and I love passing on a love for Jesus and the self-reflection part of a daily walk with Christ.

Modern lives are sterile, and the heart and soul are slowly being removed. I want to offer my gifts as a practical guide to moms, youth leaders, teachers, and whoever needs joy as I did.

Let's start investing energy, time, and passion into learning something, making something, connecting, and noticing the people and details around us. Let's invest in mindfulness and wonder without entertainment – the needless grandiose plans. Let's take a break from full-speed survival mode.

Serendipity is a word that means finding one thing when we're looking for something else.

On my journey to find relief from anxiety, seeking worth and approval from everyone around me, I discovered my calling back where I started. But I had missed it. I had missed the blessing because I was too busy looking for something of misery, something more difficult, more professional, and less frivolous. I had to give myself <u>permission to feel JOY</u>.

With that permission, I found renewed energy for art, making art, teaching art, and loving art.

Let us lay aside every weight (even the weight in our minds) that so easily besets us as scripture encourages us. We can be alert and trim our lamps without living in misery, and step into a more abundant life.

ABOUT THE AUTHOR:
Jessica Blankenship

Jessica Blankenship is an art teacher, preacher's wife, momma, and co-founder of The ARTFUL Gathering, LLC. She enjoys designing lessons and products that are both practical and inspirational, combining art, faith, and a love of learning. Jessica decided to be an art teacher when she was seven years old.

Connect with Jessica:

5

A World Where All Have Time and Space to Rest

Belinda McLean
Bendigo, Victoria. Australia.

Right from my earliest memories, work was part of life. I grew up on a dairy farm, and I used to have my naps in a cot in the milk room next to the dairy. Summer holidays always included weed control and, as I got older, tractor work and stacking hay. Did I feel 'hard done by' or overworked? No. For me, that was life.

Growing up on a farm, I had the BIGGEST backyard, which included a river that we could camp by & fish in, bushland with kangaroos, dams, secret cubbies, giant gum trees to climb, and historical ruins from a by-gone era. My love of birds, specifically eagles, came from watching a pair of wedge-tailed eagles live their lives on our farm. It was not all work; we had lots of fun, too!

My parents worked hard on our dairy farm; we had 250 cows, and we milked them twice a day. The dairy operated every day of the year, sometimes with fewer cows, but regardless, someone needed to be there twice a day, every day.

There was always an argument on Christmas Eve between myself and my sisters. Who would do the morning milking

& who would do the afternoon milking? I don't remember any physical altercations, but occasionally there were tears. We were allowed to open one present before the morning milking and the rest at 'second breakfast' after we finished the morning milking (yes, just like *The Lord of the Rings!*). So, if you were unlucky enough to be doing the afternoon milking, you not only had the later burden but also had two hours to stare at the rest of your presents while not being able to open them!! Argh!!

As a kid, I always preferred the morning milking; it was longer & more to do, but then it was over, and I felt like I could enjoy the day without the burden of a chore later on.

Spending my childhood watching my parents have to work every day of the year made me believe that you had to work hard daily to succeed. Every year mum and dad took exactly two weeks off. One week as a family and one week just the two of them. These holidays were the biggest breaks mum and dad got from the farm.

They had people they could call on to help out, both on the farm or just for milking. We hired farmhands, and as kids, we worked alongside them, chopping wood, milking cows, spraying weeds, whatever was needed. I remember my dad saying that whenever someone else milked, there were two costs; we had to pay the farmhands, and the cows would give significantly less milk (yes, stress affects cows, too!). The cost factor slightly overshadowed even our holidays.

Work was intertwined with all we did, and just like removing a piece of a puzzle, my childhood memories would be incomplete without the work. I learned that rewards came AFTER the work was done, not after a set number of hours (I still feel odd about being paid upfront for work!). I also learned that work was a part of life that constantly needed to be done, and the results of putting it aside even for a short time were expensive.

Fast forward to 2020. Living in Melbourne, we had no idea that we were in for a long haul. Over the course of the next two years, we were in lockdowns (of varying degrees) for over 260 days. Schools were conducted remotely for much of the time (2022 was the first time my girls had a full term of school since 2019!), and if I had to describe life in general, it was uncertain, exhausting, and chaotic.

My work doing live workshops stopped completely, and it wasn't long after that I felt the need to have some work in my life again. I felt like something was missing if I just sat at home all day (noting I have two younger girls, so sitting around all day was never going to happen!). I pivoted to online coaching; I ran multiple Zooms a week, and spent lots of time on social media, creating content and websites, etc. Life was busy again, with work integrated into my life.

By the end of 2020, both my husband and I had worked the whole year without taking a break. In a usual year, we have regular holidays booked with family and friends, but none of these holidays were allowed to happen in 2020, and we were exhausted.

Over the summer holidays, everyone was walking on eggshells; we weren't in lockdown specifically, but the state borders were still closed (cutting us off from family), and people were super wary about going out in groups. It felt like every break, gathering, or catch-up was a gamble. After a rocky Term 1 in 2021, New South Wales's borders opened, so we decided to go camping with my husband's family for our usual Easter break.

By this time, I had built an online presence, and every coach I learned from was saying the same thing. *"Consistency is key. You need to be continually present to reap the rewards.*

Inconsistency leads to a lack of results." There was mobile reception at the campsite, but it was slow and clunky to do anything online. And I didn't *want* to be responsible for my online presence during that time. I didn't want to show up every day; I wanted a holiday. I needed a real break.

So, I let my online people know I was taking some time off and not to expect updates for two weeks. Their response? *"Enjoy! Have fun! You deserve it."* There was a weight off my shoulders as we journeyed north.

At camp, there was the initial rush of setup, and the next day was spent trying to remember where I stashed everything and finding all the must-haves as I waded through all the stuff I now realised was probably overkill. But then the adrenalin wore off, and I found myself feeling *odd.* Like something was missing. So, I'd walk around camp, stoke the campfire, make extra trips to the creek or the shower block or anything to keep me moving, keep me *doing.*

A part of me still said that work was part of life. You need to work at *something,* anything. And so, when evaluating actions, I would give it meaning in terms of work and results (e.g., more steps = higher daily steps = a healthier lifestyle). Relaxing, chilling, and playing games felt abnormal, and it was hard just to wind down.

Our bodies are wired to react to change that's both internal (e.g., hormonal) and external (e.g., hot/cold weather). They both affect us. Our bodies react by producing, evolving, or removing a multitude of chemicals. These changes bring about physical responses to help us return to 'the norm.' When there are no changes, or it receives the same input over a long period of time, it doesn't respond; it doesn't see the need to respond. For example, when wearing clothing, your body doesn't constantly remind you, *"There's pressure on your skin everywhere!"* It ignores the constant inputs and only lets you know when your bra strap is digging in.

When we live in a constant high-stress state, our body's 'norm' is high-stress. If we take that away, our body will respond to that change and feel different. And in response, it tries to create situations to increase our stress to get it back to 'normal.' Can you see how this unbalanced process is NOT working in our favour?

For the nine months leading up to our camping trip, my norm had been a higher-stress environment; constantly changing rules, the girls at home all the time, and me trying to get an online business up and running while having a functional household. I'm sure you can see the stresses right there!

So, when I slowed down camping, my body was like, *"Where's the cortisol and adrenalin?? This feels WEIRD!!!"* It had become so used to this high-stress state that it no longer saw it as abnormal but as the norm. Ironically, I didn't *feel* stressed most of the time during the lockdown. There were definitely times that I was overwhelmed and in tears, but it was mostly just average high-stress days.

And this camping trip was less stressful than my every-day life, so my body was essentially stressed about not being stressed enough – how unfair!

I can't say I fully relaxed during that time, but I did a lot of thinking and bushwalking. Physical stress is still a stress on the body, so that alleviated my need for stress somehow! I realised that I feared letting the ball drop, slowing down, not working every day, not progressing, and that got me asking these questions:

"What if I don't start again? What if I stop and don't want to go back to work?"

I was scared.

We had a whole week of camping and then another week staying with friends. I am so grateful for this thinking time, as it gave me the space to ponder. *"So, what will I do about these questions?"* I knew I couldn't live forever in fear of *"what if?"* I had the perfect opportunity to experiment. What if I went back to work when *I* was ready, not the day after we got back (unless that's what I felt was good). I was running my own business, so I could approve indefinite leave, right?

So, I did. I started relaxing more during my holidays, and when I got back, I gave myself space & grace to see what happened.

I ended up taking just over four weeks 'off.' It wasn't that I didn't think of work or what I should be doing, but more that I gave myself space to do that thinking, pondering, and pivot my business. When I started again, I had more energy and more *desire* to be working. We were created to work; our bodies need work (in a healthy amount!) to stay agile, active, and functioning. Work is not a bad thing, but it does need to be in balance with time away from work.

And work may not be paid work; it is whatever you expend your energy on. Motherhood, exercise, relationships, and paid and unpaid labour are all work, and they need their counterbalance of rest.

After Easter 2021, I approached my work differently; I did not want to work nine months straight, then crash and burn for a month; that was not fun or sustainable. Instead, I have learned to balance my Rest And Work (RAW) rhythm. Instead of scaling cliffs and jumping off sheer drop-offs, I'd rather traverse through rolling countryside. I've made changes in my life as a whole, and I am better for it.

In 2020, I worked solidly, afraid of what taking time off would cost. So much so that I didn't even do a jigsaw puzzle. I am a HUGE fan of puzzles, from 150pc laser-cut infinity puzzles to 4000pc landscape puzzles. I love bringing order to the chaos of a box full of jumbled pieces.

But in 2020, I didn't do a single puzzle because I knew my work output would decrease while I was doing it. I'm not going to lie; I get entirely immersed in jigsaw puzzles!

After my Easter break and thinking about my RAW rhythm, I decided puzzles had to come back into my life. They were a piece of *my* life's puzzle, and without them, it was incomplete.

Movies (huge Marvel fan!!), café catch-ups & walks with friends (*with no work purpose, just fellowship*), macramé, dates with my hubby, and family outings with my girls are all things I now prioritise more as part of my RAW rhythm. I put boundaries on my work, and I'm okay with stopping for the day at lunchtime if I've done all I set out to do.

It's okay to take a break and take one often!

Everyone's RAW rhythm is different, and it changes throughout your life. I encourage you to ponder & investigate what it might look like for you.

Make sure you know what pieces are in your life's puzzle. Don't leave any pieces in the box; you can't see the finished beauty unless they are all in their proper place!

ABOUT THE AUTHOR:
Belinda McLean

B elinda McLean is an Aussie mum, author, coach, and entrepreneur. She loves adventure, pushing the boundaries, and considering the "what if...?" ideas in the entrepreneurial world. She is a math nerd and geeks out on connecting concepts to real-life scenarios to help people move forward with their goals & dreams.

Belinda loves connecting with nature through gardening, bushwalking and camping, and finds these passions refreshing & calming in the midst of the constant busyness of modern life. She advocates Rest & Work (RAW) Rhythms, and taking time out in nature to slow down and channel all those creative ideas that come when you give them time & space. She loves working with women to help them create businesses that support their goals & dreams as they enjoy their lives.

Connect with Belinda:

6

A World Where All Experience the Freedom to Create & Experience Financial Abundance

Sharlene Mohlman
Ingersoll, Ontario. Canada.

$55,000.

I added it all up, and the number just calculated over fifty-five thousand dollars. That was how much debt I had accumulated during my post-secondary education, and the number seemed so large that I would never get through it – that I would struggle forever.

Now, some of that debt level came from a little red note-book that was the bane of my existence. Starting at the ripe old age of ten years old, my step-father started documenting anything I needed or wanted that he paid for in that notebook with the expectation that I would pay it off in full. From church events that I had no choice but to attend to the carpet in my basement room, I had to pay it all back.

What I didn't know at the time was that this was a form of financial abuse, and not only was he doing it to me, but he was doing it to my mother as well. He controlled the family money and never let my mom have any, even though she was the sole provider for our family. He expected everything I used, from toilet paper to food, to be paid back to him, like I was some sort of burden rather than his child.

But I digress.

I needed to go to post-secondary education in order to better myself enough to travel to my nation's capital city, Ottawa, and serve under the presence of our Prime Minister (the same level as the President, in Canada), my dream job. I went to school and did the best that I could, both academically and financially.

Because my family was unable to support me during this venture, I accumulated a ton of debt. Credit cards, lines of credit, student loans – all increased daily until it totaled that magic number upon graduation.

I was used to not being supported financially, so it didn't really bother me. I knew I was doing the right thing, and I don't regret it whatsoever.

I was so incredibly fortunate. Without the support of any-one, I worked my butt off during my summer internships, and I managed to get my dream job! I proved I was the kind of person they needed when I graduated. Upon graduation, I landed a full-time gig, and three years later, I secured an even better gig working directly for my Prime Minister as Event Coordinator. It was a dream come true.

But I started my career plagued with debt and knew I needed to do something. All the personal finance gurus that I found suggested increasing income, and they said the only way to demolish debt was to form a side hustle or get a second job. This would be no big deal except that it was against the Accountability Act for me to have a second source of income. It was literally against the law, and although I needed more money, this job was everything I always wanted, and I needed to complete it.

I mulled the problem over and realized I wasn't the only person in this position. There were other people with lower-income jobs (because political staff got paid a *lot* less than government workers!) that couldn't have a secondary source of income. What about the disabled community, single moms, families with many children, etc.? There needed to be something for them.

That is why I developed a program that eliminated my debt in 5 years on an income of less than $50K.

Not only that, but I did it without a second income and still enjoyed my time in my beautiful nation's capital city.

The program I developed allowed me to have my coffee every day and go out for dinner once in a while. It focused on paying down my debts and enabled me to move out of my mice-infested apartment into something nicer and cleaner. But it wasn't until six years later that I realized I could share it with others.

I met an amazing mentor who taught me to believe in myself and know that I had value available that I would be able to use to impact someone else's life. I could help people like me who struggled financially and needed help. I was so excited to share what I learned in Ottawa with those that were struggling too.

It wasn't just to make money or be famous but rather to find my new passion. One that I could operate in a post-political life. I had one dream and passion for so long that when I finally achieved it, I was concerned that I would never find another passion. Through intentional work and with help from my mentor, I realized that I didn't have to have only one passion or dream for my entire life. I could add or subtract dreams at any time. I was so relieved that my change could be a tool for good that I dug deeper and realized my life's calling.

I'm here to empower women business owners to achieve financial stability and multiple income streams through effective debt demolishing and administrative services. And I am really good at these things.

I dream of a world where financial stability is a thing people don't have to long for and never achieve — one where women would feel empowered looking at their finances and not shrink back in fear. One where high income is not limited to the wealthy and anyone who wants to can eliminate their debt. These sentiments are enormous but possible when the right group of people joins forces to impact the world around them.

One of the ways I am currently empowering women is through the completion of my Debt Demolishing course. I talk about my time in Ottawa and how I managed to eliminate my debt through the program I developed for myself. Who would have thought that creating a program for myself could end up as a way to empower other women? I sure didn't at the time!

This course walks women through the entire process I completed in Ottawa with proof that it works because I did it! I discuss how facing the facts of your debt will enable you to create and understand a workable budget. In this course, flexible and fixed budget points are maximised, you track your spending to know where you are, and you don't have to have a side hustle or residual income if you can't for any reason. I encourage women to be the women they want to be; if that is a woman with her own business, then all the power to her! In this course, success is not thought to be impossible but becomes a reality.

Financial abuse happened in my life, and it happens all too often in the lives of women. The fact that I was able to overcome it proves that anyone can overcome that abuse. I dream of a world where financial abuse is not a thing, but until then, I dream of a world where women can overcome financial abuse.

I dream of a place where abundance frequently happens because small business owners know that what they are providing to their clients has huge value, and their clients love them for that. I dream of a place where women can be their authentic selves and provide resources to those in similar situations. I dream of women empowering other women to step up and operate in their gifts and then providing more resources to different people and breaking the perpetual cycle of lack because they are now in a position to empower and bless even more women.

Women are the backbones of our economy. Without them, the gifts that they possess would be missing and needed desperately. Women are our mothers, comforters, encouragers, and business owners. They possess the gifts necessary to encourage others into their own gifts. Because of the needs of women business owners, I have begun to create financial plans to help them in their personal and professional lives. They will have everything at their fingertips so that they can conquer the world, one step at a time. This action will enable women to live financially empowered and abundant lifestyles. The plans allow women to live within their means and bless others abundantly because finances in the hands of good people do good things. I believe that knowing there is support, and knowing someone is out there that has achieved financial empowerment, will give them the empowerment to live financially abundant lives.

Overall, my dreadful past has granted me the amazing experience of being able to bless lives, and I am incredibly thankful for that. I once looked at my past as something I was ashamed of, but now I see it as an example of what I can help others do. And as Robert Frost once poetically said, "that, that has made all the difference."

ABOUT THE AUTHOR:
Sharlene Mohlman

S harlene was plagued with $55k worth of debt at the ripe old age of 21. Working a job that didn't allow for multiple income streams meant she needed to figure something out. Creating a strategy that demolished her debt in 5 years on an income of less than $50K, she crushed her goals and still had money left over for fun!

Sharlene believes that financial abuse is prevalent and should be recognized so that women (for whom financial abuse is abundant) can shed their abusers and live life in financial freedom.

Sharlene now helps women achieve financial independence and abundance.

Connect with Sharlene:

7

A World Where Women Experience Childbirth as Empowering & Euphoric

Creating The Euphoric Birth Circle
Amanda Ignot
Columbia, Missouri. United States.

As a first-time mom at 37, I didn't know any way other than to follow the medical system, and the experience I had was the result of a broken system that didn't acknowledge or serve women as strong, capable beings. So many women experience their pregnancy and childbirth journey through a series of doctors' appointments, ultrasounds, and blood tests. Through this process, there are mentions of gestational diabetes, pre-eclampsia, big baby, and so many other topics meant instill seeds of doubt that illicit fear in us. These things ultimately lead women to follow the rules and do what they are told even when their gut keeps telling them something isn't right about it all.

I had to learn this the hard way. I followed the status quo throughout my first pregnancy, was belittled, bullied, and ultimately pressured into a scheduled c-section. I was told that my baby would be over 8 lbs (this is not a big baby) and that I would never be able to give birth naturally. On top of that, she was breech, and no doctors "allow" for the natural birth of breech babies. Ultimately, I agreed to the scheduled c-section, not because I thought that was best for my baby and me, but because I wanted my doctor out of my life.

No woman should have to make that decision for that reason.

Once I understood and saw my experience for exactly what it was, I knew I would never hand over that much control again. I decided to own my care. No matter what the circumstance or condition was, whether pregnancy, illness, disease, or otherwise, I would be the one making the decisions for my body and our babies. When we conceived again, I did all I could to find a doctor that would support me in having a VBAC (Vaginal Birth After a Cesarean). I knew what I wanted and wouldn't let my doctor speak doubt into any part of it. While I did find a doctor with a successful VBAC rate, I didn't feel like he was the supportive doctor I had been looking for due to his manner of care and his obvious animosity when I declined things or questioned the status quo.

Due to his manner of care and his attempt to manipulate me into a test I had declined, I knew I needed someone different. I convinced my husband that a midwife and homebirth were much better for us, and we contracted a midwife that aligned with my beliefs and believed in my VBAC vision.

I'm not going to lie, that first homebirth at forty was hard. I honestly had no idea what to expect through labor because I had never felt contractions with my first. It was intense and took all my focus and effort. Since this was my first natural birth experience, I didn't know the physiological process, and I believe that made the process much longer. Our son's birth took just over 4 hours from my water breaking to having him in my arms. Transition and pushing were the most challenging parts, but I did it on my own, with no interventions, no checks, no monitors, no tears, and no difficulties. It was so worth it! Now I understood what birth was like and had the belief that my body knew exactly what to do.

When I found myself pregnant again only eight months later, I knew I would not be seeing a doctor. We had moved and were in the process of another move in the coming months. I knew what seeing a doctor meant as far as the level of care and the doubts and limitations that would be pushed, and I wanted no part of it. I had a wild pregnancy, and it was perfect. I felt my baby growing and moving in my womb and was at peace with whatever the outcome would be.

Later in my pregnancy, I hired a midwife just for birth support, and she was the perfect person for us. As I walked through this pregnancy, I was introduced to pain-free birth, and I was all for having *that* experience; I mean, who wouldn't be, right? At the recommendation of a friend, I got the book *Supernatural Childbirth* by Jackie Mize and devoured it. I truly believed in my body's ability to grow and birth my babies, but I had no idea that it could be without pain and loved learning about trust and using the word of God and prayer to guide my experience.

It was a shock to all of us when it was time for our baby to be born. I had been praying over my labor daily for weeks, sometimes even multiple times a day. My prayer requests were for labor to be fast, easy, and pain-free. That night, while I had some contractions, they were not intense and were anywhere from 5-7 minutes apart. My husband was convinced that our baby still had weeks before she would arrive. I lay in bed and tracked my contractions as I fell asleep, then I was startled by a snap and wasn't sure if the baby had done something funny or if my water had broken. As I moved to get out of bed, there was a gush, and I knew this was it! My water had broken, and within minutes the contractions came one on top of another. We sent messages and got the midwife on her way, knowing she had to drive more than an hour to get to us.

While my husband communicated with the midwife, I was on the toilet thinking, "What in the world is going on?" But I knew in my gut that this baby was coming much faster than our last one had. Once I got off the toilet, I leaned on my husband, rocking side to side through the waves that were coming hard and fast. We had started a bath, and I was getting ready to get in when transition hit, and I roared out as I felt the baby move into the birth canal and come down. I woke the others up with that roar, and it is a good thing because they would have missed it all. As my husband walked out of the bathroom to get our 18-month-old, I heard a whisper say, "Reach down and feel." I listened to that voice and was amazed to feel her head already crowning.

I relaxed instantly, knowing she would be in my arms within a few more contractions. I got in the tub and completely relaxed, allowing my body to do all the work, and it was amazing to witness my body pushing the baby out with each contraction. I never had to help. In the next three to four contractions, she was born into my husband's hands and placed on my chest, crying that beautiful new life cry. I was in awe of what had just happened; it was less than an hour since my water had broken and I was in a haze of emotion and adrenaline.

This birth was pain-free, easy, and fast; my prayers were answered! It was euphoric as I realized and stepped into the knowledge of what my body was capable of and how strong it was, not needing any help from me pushing. My next birth at forty-three was a repeat of this one; fast, easy, and pain-free. My capable body was relaxed and knew exactly what to do once again.

When I think of birth, I envision a woman at home in a room with dim lighting instead of the harsh fluorescent lighting in a hospital, and she is surrounded by quiet, calm, and nurturing people. She is in her zone, freely moving as she wishes, eating and drinking as she needs or wants to, instead of being in a setting where she is told she can't move or eat while she labors. Nobody offers anything other than their quiet support; she is the one in charge. When she asks, they answer her every wish; they observe and wait in silence. Diffusers are running with essential oils to calm and support her, light music of her choice is playing in the background, and her other children are there showing love and excitement. She is left alone unless she asks for support instead of being continuously checked, attached to a monitor, or constantly interrupted with people in and out of her space. She has complete trust in her body, confident and calm as she moves and rolls with each new wave.

She is strong and vulnerable at the same time, focused only on the task of listening to her body and feeling her baby move down her birth canal. She is in tune with everything in and around her, knowing intuitively what to do and when to do it. There is no monitoring of fetal tones and no cervical checks unless she requests them. She trusts her instincts, knowing that her body is in complete control and doesn't need the outside involvement of those present.

It is almost time! Her baby is coming, and she is in that pivotal moment of transition where she reaches the absolute edge of her strength and belief. She cries out with a primal calling, which opens her canal a little wider, and the baby is now crowning. She allows her body to do all the pushing, leaning into the strength given to her for this purpose. She reaches down, feels her baby's head, and croons a "Hello, little one." Her husband is there holding her hand or rubbing her back, whatever she needs for support. He is prepared to be the first to touch and see their little one before handing their new love to her.

My vision for the future is one where women feel empowered and embrace their pregnancy as a natural event in life, where there isn't an unnecessary need for supervision, intervention, or control. Communities of women will come together, creating pregnancy and birth sister circles where women can learn together and support one another through their journeys. The proverbial village will return in a completely new way, giving women safe spaces to share all they are feeling and experiencing, where they can build relationships that will lift them up when they are struggling. There will be times when a woman may need a medical provider, but I believe that this need will become less and less over time as more women step into the truth of their inherent ability to grow and birth their babies. Women will glow as they share these beautiful moments with anyone who asks, and as word spreads and communities of support grow, more women will choose to have these types of experiences.

Childbirth will become an event that women walk into with confidence, expecting a euphoric experience. Their vision of childbirth will be enveloped in strength, trust, peace, joy, and serenity.

I have created a community that wasn't available when I was on this journey as a first-time mom. I provide resources, education, and empowerment to women who are going through one of the most transformative experiences of their lives. This is my calling, and I am so grateful to be able to walk beside you on your journey. Are you ready to have your Euphoric Birth experience?

ABOUT THE AUTHOR:
Amanda Ignot

A manda is a wife, mom of four, and a bestselling author who is passionate about helping women become empowered believers in themselves and their bodies. She is a pregnancy and childbirth coach with years of experience helping women through one of the most transformative times in their lives. Amanda believes every woman has the right to feel confident and capable during pregnancy and childbirth.

Connect with Amanda:

8

A World Where Children Are Deeply Cherished

Carolynn Sauer
Wichita, Kansas. United States.

The car seat had been checked and approved; our handsome little guy was strapped in with rolled blankets surrounding him for support. We were so ready to get home, sleep in our own bed, eat what we wanted to eat, have the comforts of home, and just start our lives as a family of three. But I was panicked, frozen, unable to move my feet. I just kept thinking to myself, "Wait, what?! You mean you are just going to let us leave with this tiny human? I don't get a book or a checklist or a 'how to' video? How in the world are we expected to do this?"

I was completely, utterly, gut-wrenchingly terrified, even though I felt I was someone who was 'born and bred' for being a mom (or as close as you can be). I couldn't even begin to fathom what someone who had never wanted to be a mom, someone who had never planned on being a mom, would feel in this same situation. The only thing I could think of was that maybe ignorance was bliss? You don't know what you don't know? Little did I know that this wouldn't be the last time I felt like this as a mother. My journey was just beginning.

In the song, "The Greatest Love of All," Whitney Houston sang, "I believe that children are our future." (Does anybody else have conversations and thoughts through song lyrics?) We must "treat them well and let them lead the way, show them all the beauty they possess inside." It is my dream, my wish (cue Rascal Flatts' song, "My Wish"), that children become viewed as blessings and not burdens. I want this world to regard children as Jesus did when he was here on Earth. He wanted the little children to come to Him, as the kingdom of God belongs to them (Luke 18:16). Whoever welcomes these little children, welcomes Me (Mark 9:37). Children are a blessing from God (Psalm 127:3).

For centuries, childbearing was the ultimate goal. My, oh my, have the tides turned. Now, children are seen as a burden. I remember going to my ten-year high school reunion. By this time, I already had four children. To those who knew me, this was not a big surprise. At one point in my childhood, my mom told me that I said I wanted twenty-five kids (maybe that's why I became a teacher). At my reunion, a handful of people stated that they were waiting to have kids, as they wanted to travel and focus on their careers, and they wanted the freedom to enjoy their marriage. The tone in their voices and their body language screamed that they were sorry for me. Sorry that I was already a stay-at-home mom, sorry I hadn't given myself time to travel, enjoy my marriage, and enjoy the freedom of an untethered life.

To me, though, I felt sorry for *them*. They didn't know the immense joy of the love you have for your children or the miracle a child presents to you daily as they grow and learn. They didn't know the blessed responsibility that allows you to heal your wounds and be transformed into the person God has created you to be. I already knew the incredible blessing of this love.

I have learned so much about God's love for me through loving my own children. Now that I've known this love, embraced this love, and lived this love every - single - day, I know that no matter what life throws at me or where life decides to take me, I will always know this love. When my children are grown and out of the house and I decide to focus on my career or travel, the love will go with me. I already had a jump start on this love and am so incredibly thankful that I didn't wait to embrace this most precious gift.

St. Teresa of Calcutta said, "If you want to change the world, go home and love your family." That is exactly what we need to do. We need a culture that values family again. We need to live in a world where it is possible to live with less so that we can focus on what's best. We need to make sure our children not only know that they are loved but FEEL that they are loved. Our culture values things, money, power, and prestige. It loves things and uses people, and we need to switch it back around.

Parents need the freedom from the stress of living paycheck to paycheck so that they can focus on people and relationships. They need to be able to spend quality time with their families instead of being so stressed and tired that they zone out in front of the TV, or on their phone, or both simultaneously. This zoning out screams at our children that they are less important, not worth the energy, and just a stress and a burden to us.

I believe with my whole heart that's not how most parents feel about their children. I believe that most parents really do love their children immensely but are too tired and stressed at the end of the day to show it. Actions speak louder than words, and we wind up raising humans who feel the need to succeed and produce in order to feel worthy of time and affection. In our overscheduled, overly busy world, where busy equals significance, time given also equals love and worth. We are sending our grown children into the world feeling like they have to earn love.

I know that I still have a hard time not falling into this rat race myself. This is where we need to journey together. We must latch elbows and return to the mindset of taking a village to raise a child. We need to acknowledge that motherhood is hard: back-breaking, soul-crushing, emotionally charged, knee-callusing hard. Each child is different; that's why there is no manual, checklist, or 'how to' video. We can't do it alone, nor should we, because iron sharpens iron.

We must let go of our pride and our self-sufficiency to let others see us authentically vulnerable. We must let others into our lives when we notice them breaking and then accept their support when we are on the verge ourselves. We must allow others to see our messy houses and our disheveled hearts.

Three instances come to my mind when I'm struggling with this, and it gives me the strength to continue on or allow myself to let go of my pride and accept the support. One time, one of my friends showed up at my door unannounced and at her wit's end with her children. She loves them dearly but just couldn't handle it anymore. The moment her husband walked through the door, she was out. They didn't have family in the area, and she didn't know where to go, but because I had hosted a Christmas party for Mom's Day Out, she knew where I lived. She showed up, and we sat on my front porch (away from the noise of my kids), and she talked, and we cried. We didn't solve her problems, but we were able to strengthen each other for another day. We restored courage to start again the next day.

I was able to let go of my insecurities of not having a perfectly clean, immaculate house to host the party because of another friend who was willing to be authentically vulnerable, thus making this previous situation possible. I remember we had just moved to our new house on the other side of town. I was getting to know a few ladies at church, and one of them was having a hard time. I didn't know her well at the time, but I wanted to help, so I offered to bring them dinner.

When I arrived, she welcomed me in, even though her house was in disarray. At this time, I hadn't really had many friends trust me enough to let me in (figuratively and literally) and expose their messes. Her showing me that it's OK to let people in and see your mess was such a blessing to me. Ever since, I have strived to be that person for others and allow others to be that for me when I've been in need. Most recently, they've been there for me while coming to grips with being pregnant with our seventh baby. Although I really want them and I believe that children are blessings, I was focusing on my selfishness. I wish that I didn't feel hesitant and afraid to announce our pregnancy. Once again, I wish that each child was received with rejoicing. I've felt like a hypocrite because I didn't rejoice with each of my pregnancies. I focused on myself, everything that'd be required of me to grow another child and labor them into this world. This was when my village was strong for me.

It's almost impossible to be counter-cultural on our own. Our knees will weaken, our resolve will start to disintegrate, and we will need each other to be strong when we are weak. We need to come together and take turns being strong for each other because it's hard to continue the grind when we see no progress, when we feel like a failure, or when we feel inadequate and invisible. It's a good time to remember that God doesn't call the equipped, He equips the called. I know I still need my village. So let's band together and support each other as moms. Let's be there for each other and accept help from each other.

We don't have to wait until we are all put together and know what we are doing. Even after being a mom for seventeen years to seven different humans, I'm still left panicked, frozen, unable to move my feet, second-guessing, and feeling utterly unqualified as a mother. I wonder if I'm not doing enough, doing too much, or scarring my children for life. But during some of my hardest and lowest times as a mom, I don't necessarily need a book, a checklist, or a 'how to' video. I need someone who is willing to sit with me in my mess, cry with me, and just let me know that I'm not alone in my struggles. I need someone to remind me that God gave me these children and He knows that I needed to be their mother in order for them and me to become who He created us to be. I need someone to remind me to keep the faith, have hope, and that love is enough. Let's journey together and be there for each other. Will you join me?

ABOUT THE AUTHOR:
Carolynn Sauer

C arolynn is first and foremost a child of God, a wife of eighteen years, and a mother of seven. She has four boys and three girls ranging in age from seventeen to newborn. She has a degree in Elementary Education and Early Childhood and taught preschool for five years before becoming a stay-at-home mom. Besides being a personal chauffeur to her children, she is also a Barre instructor, life coach, parent coach, author, and course creator. Carolynn loves to help guide mothers to be the best mothers they can be and is passionate about helping moms go from feeling overly busy and stressed to balanced and blessed.

Connect with Carolynn:

9

A World Where Parenting is an Invitation Into the Mysteries of Life

Parenting: An Invitation to Life
Genevieve da Silva
Port Alfred, Eastern Cape. South Africa.

H ave you ever found yourself completely drawn in and enthralled by an incomprehensible beauty or invited to a world of wonder? Have you experienced a place that seduces the senses and penetrates your perception or a moment that emancipates your emotions and directs your doings? Perhaps you viewed a work of art, an intricate mechanism, a delicate flower, a songbird's melody, or the rolling force of waves breaking against the shore.

For me, it was always the human body. Often, I would find myself on the floor of the lounge paging through the enormous grey Reader's Digest Family Medical Advisor (or something of that sort). I learnt about all sorts of things in those 600-plus pages, probably before I should have – like childbirth, for instance. No six-year-old wants to know that! Definitely not as a girl who might one day experience such atrocities to her body. But I couldn't get enough. Outstretched on the soft woollen carpet, I got lost in a world of wonder. I couldn't yet read, but I was fascinated by everything I saw. I felt the draw, the pull, the invitation to more.

As I developed reading skills, hours upon hours would be poured into searching the pages. I would stare at the pictures of how the internal structures of our body look. I would read up on how they should work, trying to make sense of the problems and solutions as explained by the symptoms and treatments suggested. To be honest, I am perplexed at how I didn't end up in the medical profession. Perhaps it was the trivially considered decision of what to study, or perhaps, as scripture says, God has directed my steps (Proverbs 16:9). What drew me in, however, time and time again, was the development of a baby in-utero and the incredible intricacy of two life forms, ova and sperm, enmeshing together to begin a journey of life for another. From what appears to be nothing comes minute webbed hands and feet, a beating heart, and an oversized alien-looking head. Slowly, as it grows from mustard seed to watermelon size, it becomes more human and recognisable. It is an incomprehensible mystery - so far beyond me and my understanding.

Life.

A wonder. A splendour. A beauty.

This elaborate mystery that cannot be grasped in its entirety continues to grip me. What is life? Where does it begin? Where does it go? When does it end? How is it that we are so dependent upon it, yet have such little control over it? The more we try to understand it, the more we are blown away by its intricacy and enormity. We pursue the preservation of it through our incredible technological advancements yet destroy it in our daily idiocies. Life enthrals me, captures my attention, and brings me to a place of whimsical fascination and curiosity. Have you perhaps experienced the thrill of such wonder?

As a child, I couldn't imagine life beyond the physical - that which lives and breathes, the body, or the physical reality. But in my trivial pursuit of a career, I veered off into the realm of the soul through psychology – the study of the human psyche. If the body is so incredibly intricate and complex, can you imagine the wonder of each unique human experience housed in the criss-cross of emotion, beliefs, personality, choice, and behaviour? The systems operating in dynamic organisation are minuscule compared to the ever-developing interaction with ourselves internally and with others around us. Here, life takes on a whole new dimension, the socio-emotional realm. One can be alive – but is one living? What does it mean to be alive – really alive? What does it mean to be? What gives life meaning? And what is the purpose of life? Is life only lived in the beautiful and positive? Is there life in despair and darkness? Can life be maximised or minimised by those I interact with? Do I alone determine what my life is? Is life really worth living? And if it is, is it meant to be lived alone or with others? And what does life with others look like?

I thought that the world of wonder that I had encountered in the soul was extensive and that life - the human experience - would be something that could keep my curiosity enthralled. But then I discovered more. Can you see my inner child leaping and giggling? Is yours? Can you see her eyes wide and her smile stretched in absolute delight? Can you see her eyes twinkle and her mind race to keep up with her heart?

There is life that begets life; life that continues and flows and never runs out. There is unexplainable, incomprehensible, unmeasurable, uncontainable life; an experience of the mystical that words cannot express, where heaven meets earth and all that was perfect is perfect again. John, an apostle of Jesus, described a moment in time when a woman met a man, and everything changed. At a well outside a town, alone, afraid, and ashamed, she met the One who gives life that flows like springs of living water. In an instant, everything changed, and she ran and shouted to all who would listen, "Come and see..." (John 4:29, NLT). John described over and over how people encountered Jesus and ran to find whoever would listen, then invited them to "Come and see." Even the disciple Peter, when given the option to leave, exclaimed, "But Lord, where would we go? No one but you gives us the revelation of eternal life." (John 6:68, TPT) Life begins in the natural realm, but there is an invitation to life beyond the natural – a wading deeper and deeper into the source of life and encountering Him and all that He is, allowing him to transform that which is natural.

Life, true life!

One who has never experienced it thirsts deeply for it. One who has experienced it cannot fathom being separated from it.

I am a professional in the world of parenting and family. But I am also a sojourner in this same world, trying to figure out what it means for myself and my boys. I have spent years studying, writing theses, producing helpful tools, and conducting therapy sessions around the theories of healthy family functioning. But I have spent hours upon hours berating myself, holding myself up to the unreachable expectation of being the perfect parent. I have cried so many tears as I see that what I have suggested to others, I cannot even master myself. I recount and relive the dreadful moments in the middle of the night when I lost all sanity and could not attend to my child with love but with emptiness and distance. I have moments of hope when I see that some task or chore is becoming a norm. I breathe a sigh of relief when I no longer have to be up first on a Saturday to ensure the house isn't destroyed in boisterous chaos and excitement for life. And I smile, deeply overwhelmed with gratitude, as I receive love in all its various forms from these little ones who, for some reason, think that this broken, fallible, messed-up human being is the best thing in the whole wide world. What has been so fascinating to examine, read, explore and wonder about in books and in my mind has shaken and rivalled the most desperate inadequacy in the reality of living it out.

Life, so complex, mysterious, enthralling, and immense, is housed in the tiniest of persons and given to us to steward and raise. This is a concept so far beyond me. It is overwhelming – but so inviting. It is so unfathomable – yet so simple. It is so auspicious – yet taken for granted. Why does the creator of life entrust life to us when we have such capacity to destroy life? No wonder parenting stretches us beyond what we can naturally manage. While becoming a parent may start in the physical, being a parent must transcend to something far greater. I have discovered that keeping the body alive is achievable – to some extent. Breathing life into the soul is complex, but a heritage of research and theory offers accessible implementation. But it is life in the spirit that is beyond me. And yet, it is this life that makes all the difference, at any moment, in every human experience, now and eternal. And I find that this is where the overwhelming fear of failure and the indistinct reality of my inadequacy is either exacerbated or silenced.

I have been on a journey these last few years where God has had to arrest me in my struggle to achieve the unachievable standards I had set in my mind as a parent. He has had to arrest me in my performance of perfectionism and bring me to the backstage of my brokenness. It is in this place where he has met with me and loved me. It is here in the hidden darkness where I have encountered his divine light. And it is in this place where I have surrendered what is dead to find the life that only comes when I am with Him. I cannot love without his love. I cannot be patient without his patience. I cannot hope without his hope. I cannot steer towards a future without his future. My friend, I have all the knowledge and skills that should make stewarding my children's life a breeze – but they are not enough, and I will never be or have enough. And I have had to accept that this is OK. There is a source of life that is deeply needed, that transcends these other areas and creates something that cannot be explained. It is beyond me. And it is what my children really need.

My prayer for my children is now simply, "Jesus, may my children encounter you and choose to pursue you at a young age. Help me to direct them to you." If He is the source of life, then my efforts will never be enough. But I can be the conduit that allows my children to encounter the source. The Passion Translation of Ephesians 6:4 shifted everything for me when it came to being a parent. "Fathers, don't exasperate your children, but raise them up with loving discipline and counsel *that brings the revelation of our Lord.*" (Italics mine). For so long I have seen parenting as the extension of myself into the future. How am I raising my children so they may be responsible contributors to society? But this invitation by the apostle Paul shifts everything. If my children discover life itself – overflowing, abundant, 'steams of living water' life – then their lives will be an abundant outflow of that life, bringing life to others. Why does the creator of life entrust life to us when we have such capacity to destroy life? Could it be that the creator of life invites us to the source of life to experience life and reproduce life - generation, after generation, after generation? "Be fruitful and multiply." (Genesis 1:28, NLT) Could our call to produce life perhaps be a call, not only of the physical and psychological, but more so, the eternal? This call to multiply life in the garden, where perfection and proximity in His presence was the reality, came after he breathed life into man – His life in us. His image in us shows us who we truly are.

Parenting may start in the physical realm. It most definitely develops into a socio-emotional maze – complex, unique, mysterious, but manageable, systematic, and doable. But there is a transcendent level, which is beyond us all, to which we are all invited. We are invited to explore, experience, and become utterly enamoured with life. We are invited to life beyond life; for our generations to experience life. How will you respond to the invitation?

ABOUT THE AUTHOR:
Genevieve da Silva

D r. Genevieve da Silva (D.Ed) works in the fields of mental health, family relationships, and childhood development. She is passionate about rebuilding healthy families, equipping children for their future, and awakening hope in others. As an Educational Psychologist, she consults, educates, and trains current and future parents, teachers, and mental health professionals. Genevieve is married to Rick da Silva, and together they are raising their three boys in the beautiful and diversity-rich Republic of South Africa.

Connect with Genevieve:

10

A World Where Education Systems Prepare Children for Purpose & Calling

Lydia Eppic
Memphis, Tennessee. United States.

I am sitting in my office at school, reflecting on a truly memorable day. We are in midday rest time, and everything is quiet.

The kettle gently whistles, letting me know my tea is ready. I get up and slowly pour a cup into my favorite lighthouse mug. "Find Your Purpose, Shine Your Light," it says.

That's exactly what I witnessed today.

As I settle back into my favorite chair with my mug in hand, I feel warm inside even though I haven't taken a drink. I take a long sip of my tea, breathe in deeply, and exhale slowly.

My eyes lovingly scan the photo collage corkboard hanging across from my desk. I see pictures from the first schoolhouse, creator projects from the previous summers, children's dream board sketches, and lots of joyful, smiling faces. I smile back.

Many days I wonder if the sacrifice and work of parenting are worth it, especially when swimming upstream against the culture around me. Yet today was proof that all the years of early mornings, tough conversations, and long drives were not in vain.

Let me explain.

An old proverb says, "Train up a child in the way he should go, and when he grows up, he will not depart from it." For most of my life, I read that proverb thinking it meant that a parent's responsibility is to control their children: to raise their kids with good manners, teach them how to say their prayers, be good taxpayers, and decent spouses and humans. That children are objects to be controlled that will one day grow up to control their children. And the cycle perpetuates.

Yet one day, I reread that same proverb with fresh eyes and realized the writer wasn't talking about creating a colony of mini-mes. In fact, this statement was not about me being in control at all. It was about me making the tough, scary, yet vitally important choice to *release* my control. Completely.

This proverb is a powerful universal law – a cause and effect:

CAUSE: Train up a child in the way they should go, teaching them to seek God's wisdom and will for their abilities and talents . . .

EFFECT: And when they are old, they will not depart from it. (Proverbs 22:6 AMP)

This begged the question in my mind.

So what happens to the child who doesn't learn to develop their abilities and talents?

It leads to an adult without a clear direction of their purpose and calling.

They struggle to find their unique path, consumed by keeping up with culture, appearing normal, and trying to blend in and fill a role that was never meant for them.

They are left struggling, confused, frustrated, and hopeless.

I was speechless. We were all *missing* it. For generations of westernized evangelical culture, we totally missed the mark.

This same law, when applied correctly, can lead to generations walking confidently and boldly in their purpose and calling – a calling beyond good grades, accolades, and awards – beyond impressing their peers and amassing bragging rights for their parents.

This law applied correctly means that discovering your purpose goes from being an enigma to the daily guiding compass of life.

I had spent so many years of my own life feeling adrift and without that compass. After choosing to leave my fast-growing engineering career to become a homemaker, I felt an extreme loss of identity. My work was my life; without the accolades and encouragement to motivate me, I felt lost and discouraged.

I was desperate for clear direction and tried to be like the perfect, pretty, side-hustling moms I saw all around me. Yet no matter what I did or tried, my efforts to conform and be like them felt forced. I had given up on being myself because I had no idea what being me meant! I just wanted to throw myself into a job, make some money, and cover up the gaping hole of insecurity and hopelessness. Yet I wanted so much more for my own children.

That revelation led to a search – a hero's journey. And on that journey, it was my children who prompted me to consider other ways to approach the root of my story: education. I went to public school myself and did well, yet I had this uneasy feeling we needed to give our kids another way to grow and learn. I later taught at both a brick-and-mortar school and with homeschool families and noticed the stark difference in ability and time to help children develop into their own person.

But how in the world would I do it when I had no idea how to teach small kids?? That question led to an unexpected process of unlearning and relearning. I desired a whole-child education that helped my own children connect with their purpose and celebrate their unique design – I was determined to find it.

My husband and I dreamed of an environment that would foster and develop their God-given genius.

So we did the uncomfortable, the unconventional, and the unglamorous.

We hybrid-homeschooled and drove hundreds of miles weekly to give them the learning center they needed. We gave up the need to be in control and started searching for our Creator-given purpose. I first apprenticed at Ivy Greene Academy in Pontotoc, Mississippi, and received mentorship from The Tinkering School in San Francisco, two learner-led, project-based schools. We started to forge a new path.

With the encouragement of my mentors, we explored the notion of what happens when you give children the space to express and discover their unique creativity.

Our secondary mission? Train children up in their inherent gifts and talents, their driving purpose in the world.

But this education revolution isn't just for young adults.

My primary mission is to transform generations of *parents* to live out their unique God-given purpose, free from insecurity and constant stress.

This brings me to the event earlier today.

The alumni reunion breakfast was beautiful. I witnessed a collection of recent graduates, seasoned entrepreneurs, and business leaders networking and celebrating a nonprofit margin fundraiser.

The alumni of our program are pursuing their purpose through their unique abilities and talents. They are thriving in their callings and personal lives – growing with their Creator and trusting Him with their life and their process. Some are slowly finding their way; others are in full bloom – each one right on time.

It was such a joy to see them. They are like my own family. I remember their stories and stand in awe of their glow.

These are the kids who were different and felt bullied by a system that didn't understand them. When I say bullied, I don't mean simply bullied by other kids because of their personality, quirks, or size. I mean bullied by teachers and administrators who didn't understand their special and unique qualities.

In the old definition of 'training a child,' they were pressured, overlooked, or shamed into conformity. This system is ruled by control only to promote the characteristics that make their school look good, their families look good, and their paychecks match, without any thought for the Creator's wisdom, their abilities, or their talents.

Not on my watch.

At our center, these children found a community that believed in them. They realized that their desire to feel accepted started with themselves, and with encouragement and guidance, the rest would follow. The parents were, of course, encouraged by the changes they saw. Their children were healing – opening up, showing courage, and taking creative risks.

Going against the grain is not easy and is definitely an invitation for ridicule and scorn. I remember that some of our families received a lot of pushback from others in their families when they enrolled. They didn't understand why they needed to be so 'different.' The truth is many of these bright young minds were being snuffed out in the traditional education system. Our school is a place where they get to shine fully and bravely, many for the first time in their lives.

Many of the alumni at the breakfast chose to go to trade school. In some cases, they did go to college because they had a particular calling on their life to pursue that area of expertise. These young men and women pursued apprenticeships and trade school, developed their skills, and found joy and satisfaction in their work. They found purpose and cultivated laser focus on what they're called and created to do. This secret has led them to become unusually successful at such a young age.

As I reflect on the faces I saw at breakfast, this is what I see:

I see the hyperactive child who overcame crippling social anxiety.

I see the quiet empath who creates evocative artwork through code.

I see thriving young adults, some quiet, some bold, some hilarious, all expressing their unique voices in an environment of acceptance and celebration – a colorful and supportive cocoon.

What moved me most was not the testimonials or the goals achieved. You could see it, feel it in the atmosphere. The whole room was filled with transformed hearts.

It wasn't just the students who had transformed. The obvious transformation in the hearts and minds of the parents was even more astounding.

Most parents would say they are willing to do anything for their children.

But there's one thing 99% of parents aren't willing to give up – *control*.

These parents are the 1% who were brave enough to go through the painful yet gloriously freeing process of unlearning everything – and I mean everything – they believed about life and work and what culture taught them was true. They were brave enough to let go of their ego and their preconceived notions, rediscover their purpose, and embrace their true calling in their everyday lives.

They released the need to be in control and, with childlike faith, began to seek God's wisdom for their abilities and talents – a process that was misused or abused when they were children. These men and women chose to give up control for the sake of their children and their children's children.

This paradigm shift allowed them to establish an environment for their children to thrive in every area of their lives, not just at school.

People often think that a child's scholastic achievement is the sole responsibility of the school. "I send them to school, and the school and the teachers take care of their education. As a parent, I'm basically just housing and feeding my kid until they wake up and do it all over again," for eighteen long years.

So we asked, "What if there was a way to change the narrative? What if we empowered parents to confidently engage in their children's learning by modeling learning and transformation in their own lives?"

The result was our unique center – a place of discovery, risk, exploration, and purpose for students and parents alike.

Our students spend the majority of their time at home, and their parents are transformed alongside them. These mothers and fathers are willing to unlearn everything they know about what it means to live with purpose. And now, a new legacy of learning begins in each brave family.

I take another sip of tea. Midday rest is almost over, and I can feel the gradual rise in energy on the campus. Reflection time is coming to an end. Soon we will be back to doing the good work. Now is the time.

ABOUT THE AUTHOR:
Lydia Eppic

L ydia is an Amazon best-selling author, lifestyle coach, speaker, and advocate of thriving families. Her mission is to help working moms from all walks of life discover their unique brand of joy and fulfillment.

She is a thought catalyst and creator of Spark!, a workshop to help women rediscover their 'why' hidden in their personal stories.

Lydia lives outside Memphis, TN, with her amazing husband and two Young Creators.

Connect with Lydia:

11

A World Where Families Are Incubators of Purpose & Calling

Checklists, Communication, and Catharsis
Laurie Bene
Windsor, Ontario. Canada.

"And he will turn the hearts of the fathers to the children and the hearts of the children to their fathers, lest I come and strike the earth with a curse." NKJV Malachi 4:6

One day my son came home from a day of school in the second grade looking so sad and disappointed. He stopped right in front of me, his big blue eyes welling up with tears and his gaze focused on the floor. He stood in silence, making me wonder if he had gotten into trouble or what was going through his little seven-year-old mind. I waited a minute and then questioned him about what it was that seemed to have him so upset. He slowly moved his focus from the floor to me and then shared his disappointment. In his class that day, they had been talking about what they wanted to do when they grew up. At this point, his head dropped again, and he sniffed, "I don't know what I can do because I'm not good at math." Math, I thought, that is what has my sweet boy so concerned.

Wow, this was already important to me, but now it was even clearer. When I saw the disappointment on his face and knew what little bearing second-grade math had on his potential for success in life, I knew I needed to find the proper support system for him. Also, giving him what was missing in a public school setting became very important. I had not felt a prompting to homeschool, but at times I did envy those who did because they could teach to their children's strengths. That became a priority for me. Although my children were in the public school setting, I would be sure to understand who they are, how they work best, and help them discover their gifts, their passions, and what they were created for. This does not always look like what society has created for us to be boxed in to. My definition of success is likely much different than that of North American society at large.

As a Mom of two teens and someone who has been in contact with many kids in my career, I have noticed this is an area where kids seem to be struggling. They lack the clarity of where they truly excel and what giftings they possess. They cannot find what they were created for without seeing that first. I truly believe communication and a true connection with us are two essential factors in them discovering where they shine.

When I look around and see where society has landed the family, my heart is saddened. I don't know about you, but I see plenty of people every day rushing from here to there. This parent headed this way and the other that way, each trying to split themselves in two, and that's just to get the kids dropped off to the first commitment of the extracurriculars for the day.

What if there was a way we could do things differently?

How would our families and parenting look if:

-We did not feel we had to keep up with the Jones.

-Each of us was confident enough in who we were meant to be that we didn't feel pressured to do things we were not truly passionate about.

-We were fulfilled and did not feel the need to constantly rush from this sport or hobby to another to be validated.

-We knew what our children's strengths and passions were and encouraged them to pursue that which would be life-giving for them.

-Our children did not feel they had to fit into some mold to be accepted.

So often, I wonder if we have these checklists in our minds that we feel need to be completed to 'succeed' as a family today.

- Honor roll
- Travel teams
- Enriched classes
- All city sports
- 'Cool' friends
- The best school
- Straight 'A' report cards

Are these checklists really even ours to begin with? Are we striving to live up to someone else's ideals and pressures? Who are we doing this for? Is it truly what we desire for ourselves – for our kids?

I believe it is time for families to take a good, close look at where they are going to get really clear on what matters to them as a family. What serves your family well? What are your hopes, dreams, and ambitions as individuals and together? The things you CHOOSE to surround yourselves with should ultimately support those priorities. Not everything we do lines up perfectly. However, we can approach decision-making through the lens of how it aligns with our family's passions and goals rather than, "What will others think?" or "How can I keep up with what everyone else is doing?" This would make it so much easier to say "No" to something that deep down wasn't your desire or theirs to begin with. What would it be like to have a schedule that is less hectic and more rewarding? What would it be like if we felt more fulfilled at the end of the week, month, or year because those things we <u>choose</u> to do are actually satisfying our deepest desires?

Connecting is key if we desire to better understand our children and their gifts, passions, and dreams. Communication and being present are essential factors in getting to know who they really are. We have so many advances in technology that make communication readily available. We are able to 'talk' any time of day, yet we are becoming more disconnected. Our families should be the first place we know we have clear and open communication.

My heart breaks when I see a family out for dinner 'together,' but they all have devices in front of their faces and are not interacting with each other. How can we know each other and grow as a family if we don't even take the time to talk over dinner? That is a perfect time to catch up on everyone's day and possibly even talk through some concerns that need to be addressed. Communication is imperative to know each other well. We must be intentional and take the time to learn who our children are, understand how they think, and know what is important to them. Watch and learn what makes them smile, what lights them up, and what their strengths are. In turn, we can help them see those things as well.

I have had many conversations with young people who were about to graduate from high school and had no idea what they wanted to do for 'the rest of their lives.' Many of them had spent hours every week in an arena, gym, or field – so much so that they decided on their own they had had enough and stopped playing altogether. Don't get me wrong, I love sports and all they have to offer, but a very small percentage of our kids will play at the professional level. I wonder if many of them have a false hope of what it may become for them. If we invested even a portion of that time into understanding the rest of who they are, I truly believe many kids would have a clearer picture of where they were headed as they neared graduation.

We often don't see the very things that are our strengths, we may realize the things we enjoy or what we prefer to spend time doing, but others often help us see the gifts we possess. We often can't see the forest for the trees in our own lives. Who better to pour into our children's, teens', and young adults' lives than us? Who better to see their potential? It is great to hear from others, but if we are all honest, I am sure there is a longing in our hearts around having our parents tell us the potential they see or have seen in us. We have the ability to make this happen for our own children. Although we may not have received this ourselves, that should make us desire it all the more for them.

How can we make that happen?

First and foremost, we *must* take the time to know them, really know them. As we see the areas where they shine and encourage them in those giftings, it helps to get practical. Get past the screens and how-to videos and try to make it experiential; learning through technology is great, but nothing is better than boots on the ground. Help them find opportunities to try what interests them and what excites them. You never know what those opportunities may lead to.

I know communication can be a process, a difficult one for some, especially depending on past communication or lack of it. But in my experience, typically, if we truly show interest and respect for our kids, they will be willing to share with us. Respect is a two-way street; if we want to be respected, we must also show it to them.

We can also improve communication by working through our own emotional trauma from past issues. As we tackle these areas, we become better versions of ourselves and less likely to be triggered when we have difficult situations arise with our children. We become more capable of responding to issues rather than reacting to them. As we deal with them, it may help us to realize similar patterns in our kids' behavior. When we are aware, we can get them any help they might need to work through it.

Working toward our own emotional healing will allow us to communicate much more calmly even if/when an issue arises. We often think we have worked through something only to see it appear time and time again. Healing is a process, but there is a way to get to the root of the issues rather than just covering them with a band-aid. There are patterns with a root of emotional trauma that keep plaguing our families. What if we could turn that around? What if we created a legacy that went in the opposite direction? Once we see these patterns for what they are and have the tools we need to work through them, we can stop the cycle and see a change from the downward spiral of these generational issues.

Our children may also be dealing with areas of emotional trauma. One common issue many have dealt with is being bullied. Unfortunately, this is all too common and will typically need to be worked through, or it will have long-lasting effects. We all know kids can be cruel, but sometimes, although it may not be commonly viewed as bullying, it may be at the hands of an influential adult. A teacher, for example, who speaks negative words can have a lasting effect on a child and how they move forward in life.

Just a side note, a great teacher can also leave words on a child's heart that will positively influence them for the rest of their life. Our family has experienced both sides of this coin.

As we have helped our children work through these things, we have seen a change in them, so they do not have to spend as much time working through these issues and all that comes with them. They more easily recognize what is happening if they have the tools to work through it. If something becomes visible to them, they can more quickly identify it before it affects them deeply and, in turn, change their legacy.

I can't help but smile when I think about how the family dynamic could change if we really had a handle on these areas. What would our homes be like? What would our world be like?

Imagine living your life in your own lane as a family – a life where you and those closest to you no longer feel overwhelmed by the constant rush and comparison to those around you. You are no longer fighting to live up to a 'dream' that deep down you know is not yours, to begin with. You live a life where your kids' first thought when they are struggling with something important or need someone to talk to is to *come to you* because they know you are a safe place. They know you are there for them; you know them better than anyone else on this earth. The only one who knows them better is their Creator. Imagine knowing you have the tools and support you need if and when you or your kids need emotional healing and restoration, and you can confidently move forward to the place you were meant to be—each living out their passion and purpose.

This is my Heaven on Earth.

ABOUT THE AUTHOR:
Laurie Bene

Laurie Bene is a wife and Mom from the deep south of Canada, :) Windsor, Ontario. She is a heart-centered Life Coach and an Anointed to Soar Emotional Healing Coach who has a passion for helping parents empower their kids to find their potential and purpose.

While building her business to impact families, Laurie has also been employed as a Dental Hygienist for 25 years, where she has grown skills in quickly diffusing emotional situations with children from a young age to adulthood. She is now taking this valuable experience into her world of coaching to assist parents in this sometimes difficult arena, which lights her up as she loves to see kids and youth thrive in their well-being.

A verse that has become a driving force for her is Ephesians 2:10, "For you are God's Masterpiece, created in Christ Jesus to do good works, which God prepared in advance for you to do."

Connect with Laurie:

12

A World Where Women Are Supported Regardless of Their Career Choices and Vocation

Paula Henry
Columbia, Maryland. United States.

I remember it like it was yesterday. I was standing in an alcove at work, looking out the glass doors to the parking lot. I didn't want to be there. I wanted to be home with my kids. I felt like I had been punched in the gut. What was this feeling? Where was it coming from? I had a career that I loved and great people that I worked with, yet, I felt the tug in my heart to be home with my kids. I pushed the feeling away.

My father died unexpectedly when I was 8, which left our family without financial stability. From a young age, my mother instilled in us the importance of going to college and having a career. No matter how tight money was, she prioritized our education because she believed education was the key to success. We attended a local private school with significant financial aid, and we never talked about "if I go to college," instead, we spoke about "when I go to college." She wanted us to be strong, independent women, capable of supporting

91

ourselves no matter what life threw at us. She wanted more for us than the life she had.

I focused on doing well in school and finding a career that would be challenging and rewarding. In high school, I met a child with a cochlear implant, and I was fascinated. I took classes in American Sign Language and cued speech, and I was hooked. From that point on, I was determined to work with individuals with hearing loss and pursued a career as an audiologist. I put my head down and my blinders on – full speed ahead to a fulfilling career. There was no room in my plan for children. Clinical work as an audiologist led to a passion for research, leading to another graduate school round. Once I was in my post-doctoral fellowship, I finally allowed myself to begin dreaming about my future beyond my career. I was surprised to find a deep desire for a family of my own.

My husband and I decided to start a family and were elated when I quickly became pregnant. My first delivery was traumatic, and it took quite a bit of time for me to recover. As a new mom, I was lost. It's one of the few times I felt a lack of control in my well-planned life. My hormones were raging, and all I wanted to do was run away. We had no family nearby; we felt so isolated. Through support from friends, I plodded through maternity leave but was anxious to return to work.

I only took eight weeks of maternity leave. I found an in-home daycare just a short drive from our house, and my son seemed happy there. I jumped back into auditory research with a passion. Along came our second child and a similarly traumatic delivery. This time, I wasn't as anxious to return to work. Was it because I was exhausted from caring for two children under the age of three? Perhaps. In hindsight, I think my heart was being pulled toward staying at home. My job was a sixty-mile drive away, so I was not looking forward to returning to that commute. I was exhausted, but again, I put my blinders on and plodded ahead.

The next year brought a move to a new city, resulting in a longer commute and the loss of the support network I had painstakingly built. I found a fabulous in-home daycare in our neighborhood, and the kids thrived. My stress over ensuring they were well taken care of during the day was reduced, knowing they were happy and in good hands.

When my son started Kindergarten, our schedule grew more challenging, but I was determined to make it work. In the spring of that year, things reached a boiling point. I was so exhausted that I knew something had to give. It took a lot of courage, but I walked into my boss' office and asked if I could scale back to working part-time. I felt as if I was in a tug of war with my career. We shifted to living on my husband's salary as an experiment. We put my salary in the bank in preparation for leaving my job if that's what I chose to do.

With the support of my boss and some very nimble scheduling, I was able to make it work. Some days I was working from home, other days, I went into the office, and still others, I was off completely. I hired a fantastic college student to help fill in the gaps with childcare. The hardest days for me were the ones when I left the house before the kids were awake. That really pained me. I wanted to be there for the bookends of the day – getting them up in the mornings and tucking them in at night.

My son started bringing home homework, as all kids do. There were days when his homework would be done before I got home. His nanny was helping him with it. She had the best of intentions, but it was yet another thing that hurt. I was supposed to be the one working on it with him. I felt like a rag doll being pulled apart. I wasn't giving enough to anyone. When I was at work, my mind was on things at home, but when I was at home, there were times I wanted to be at work. I remember getting a call from the school nurse while I was at work. My daughter was running a fever and needed to be picked up. I informed her I would be there in an hour – that was the fastest I could get there. She let out an exasperated sigh and asked if there was any way I could get someone else there sooner. The guilt was overwhelming. I wanted to curl up under my desk and cry. I was trying to do the best for my kids, and my best wasn't good enough. That phone call was a wake-up call. I needed to do what was best for my kids, at least for now.

I felt nauseated as I prepared to tell my boss. We had discovered that we could, in fact, make ends meet on my husband's salary alone. When I finally told my boss that I needed to resign, he was incredibly understanding. He commented that he was surprised I had lasted as long as I had, knowing how long my commute was.

I was about to leave my career and was scared out of my mind. I protected myself by choosing to view it as a temporary thing. I'd be back, I told myself. When my coworkers threw a going-away party, and one of the managers referred to it as my retirement, I shook my head in disbelief – no, this wasn't retirement, just a temporary break. The sentiment stung. I was coming back someday, not retiring.

My kids were 8 and 6 at the time. I remember the drive home that day, crying for my loss. It was Halloween, and I went out trick-or-treating with my kids, trying to be present and enjoy the fun with them. This was just a temporary change for me; I wasn't yet willing to leave my career completely. For five years after leaving my job, I kept up my certifications and continuing education. Time and money that I could have spent elsewhere were spent on my career with the intent that I would return because I wasn't willing to let go.

For five years, I lived in a state of limbo, thinking I would return someday. In hindsight, I went through all five stages of grief (denial, anger, bargaining, depression, and acceptance). My denial prevented me from making any long-term plans for myself or my family. I was biding time before I could go back to my career. Holding on to the hope of returning to work prevented me from being fully present for my kids.

There were many blessings that came from me leaving my career, such as being able to spend time with my mother when she was diagnosed with pancreatic cancer, but there were challenges and guilt too. I didn't have a network of moms to hang out with while my kids were at school during the day, and it was really challenging to make connections. I relied on my involvement in a quilting guild to help me navigate this new life. Ultimately, I was both scared and grateful. I was scared that I would find myself resenting my kids, yet grateful that I could be there for them in their formative years. I was incredibly thankful to be able to spend time with my mother during her illness and treatment. I took several trips down to Virginia to take her to her treatments and just to visit. There was no way I would've been able to take time off to do that if I was still working. But, deep down, I was angry about leaving my career, and it took everything in me not to take it out on my kids. I had worked so hard for my career, and now it was gone.

I felt guilty for not contributing to our household income, so I got a job at the school as a lunch and recess monitor. This was part of the bargaining phase for me. The job didn't pay much, but it made me feel useful. It also helped me make some adult connections, which made me feel less isolated. I missed the stimulating conversations with co-workers, the lunches out, and the laughter. I couldn't stomach the notion that I was JUST a stay-at-home mom. I was still so deep in denial that I would introduce myself by telling people what I used to do. It took a long time for me to willingly say, "I stay at home with my kids."

After my mom died, depression rolled in like storm clouds. The loss of my mother folded into the loss of my career, and I found myself enveloped in darkness. The final stage of grief is acceptance, which took me nearly five years to enter. Acceptance is a process and not a destination. I continue to work towards full acceptance, but I may never reach it. There will always be the loss of what I thought my life would be like. Instead of spending so much time in denial of my new phase of life, I wish someone had told me that it was okay to be sad and angry over the loss of my career. Even a transition into something good and wanted can be full of grief over what we are leaving behind. Resisting grief is resisting growth. Finally accepting my new identity as a stay-at-home-mom allowed me to fully grieve what I was leaving behind and embrace my future with newfound hope.

As a society, I would like to see moms be less judgmental of each other. There's a battle going on between career moms and stay-at-home moms, each judging the other. Career moms view stay-at-home moms as wasting their potential, and stay-at-home moms view career moms as not spending enough time with their families. In reality, there's not one perfect way to be a mom. You can be a career mom, or you can be a stay-at-home mom, and each is equally valuable.

For moms choosing to leave their careers and stay at home with their families, I want them to have a smooth transition. They need to be aware that they're entering the battleground between career moms and stay-at-home moms. To have a smooth transition, they must acknowledge the need to grieve the loss of their career as the life they thought they would have and embrace the new stay-at-home mom life that's before them. I know that if I had actively embraced the grieving process over the loss of my career, my transition to stay-at-home mom life would have been easier and faster. It took me 5 or 6 years to complete the grieving process, which is far too long. I missed out on some valuable moments with my kids because I was in the mindset that this stay-at-home mom life was temporary. Now that I have reached the stage of acceptance, my kids benefit from a mom enjoying being present in their lives, and I'm confident that I made the right decision for me.

Once I shifted my mindset, my kids noticed. I wasn't stressed about taking care of them anymore, and I wasn't biding my time. I shifted my mindset from "I have to" to "I get to," and it has made all the difference. I have become a calmer, more patient mom, and being fully present in my family's lives helps me fully enjoy my time with them.

I became a certified life coach in 2021. Now, I help other moms choosing to leave their careers and transition to stay-at-home mom life. Using what I've learned along the way to help others find their individual path is incredibly fulfilling. I want every mom to enjoy the time she has with her kids. The time is so short. Motherhood is a complicated journey. We grow, we shrink, we break, we heal. The expanding and shifting are where the beauty happens, here in the messy middle.

ABOUT THE AUTHOR:
Paula Henry

Paula Henry is a woman of many talents. She worked for the Department of Defense for ten years as a Research Audiologist before deciding to leave her career to stay at home full-time with her kids. Transitioning from career mom to stay-at-home mom was a challenge but ultimately proved to be a fulfilling journey. Now, as a life coach, she uses her wit and wisdom to help other women make the same transition she did. She lives in Maryland with her husband, two kids, and a Dalmatian who loves her dearly.

Connect with Paula:

13

A World Where Grace is Given Freely

A Piece of Heaven on Earth
Ruth Sierra
Waco, Texas. United States.

My take on Heaven on Earth:
"*In the beginning* ...."

When this is uttered or thought, the words after it fall into their place quite naturally. "God created the heavens and the earth." Absolutely nothing was lacking in His magnificent creation.

Walk with me and be mesmerized by the creation story, as found in Genesis, Chapter 1. I imagine the light, the separated spaces, the earth and the heavens, the dry and wet grounds, and the vegetation of every kind – perfect for all lives. I see all the animals made by God, the fish in the waters, the birds in the skies, the livestock, and the wild animals that scurry along the ground, woven by Him and brought to life. Best of all, I see the human!!

I imagine the Garden of Eden like this:

There was a beautiful sunset with a flowing river reflecting the golden rays of sunlight. The water flowed through with a soothing sound as the birds chirped in the trees. Animals walked by, and Adam hand-fed them. Eve held her husband's hand and gazed at the sunset, longing for nothing, feeling absolute peace and contentment in the most perfect place on Earth.

There were colors that the human mind could not imagine, and beautiful flowers spread across the banks of the river. They felt a gentle breeze, the fresh fragrance of earth like a newborn baby, and God was watching from afar, smiling on them and blessing them. Adam ran to His Father like a child when he had a question because there was free access between God and Man.

God was walking in the midst of his creation on earth. We can rephrase this as God living with his creation, or 'Heaven on Earth' – the purest form of love. Everything God created, He handed to man. God put unrelenting trust in mankind when He just gave the entire earth to them. Sometimes, this thought suffocates me.

How would man in his small mind ever grasp the fullness of God's creation and the intricate details to be managed? Even though it is man's responsibility to watch and take care of everything, my inner being tells me to trust God. He made this world in a self–sustaining fashion. God did not create man to hand him a job. He created Man to enjoy all the creations. That is why God made man last – after He perfected everything else. However, God already knew the disasters man could and would cause within His creation.

The Rift Between God and Man

After Adam and Eve ate the forbidden fruit, God parted from man's company. That was God saying, "You have now disobeyed me, and you are not in unison with me." (Read John 15: 4-11). Then man was sent out of Eden. He still had access to all of creation, except the Creator Himself. And that's how we lost Heaven on Earth. To have Heaven on Earth simply means 'God himself with us.'

This distance that Satan has caused between God and man is the opposite of Heaven on Earth, and it limits the true capability of man's heart to love God like God loves man. Sin entered the world and formed its roots in man's heart and mind. It started with a lie, then a murder, and another lie, followed by a curse, as the offspring of Adam and Eve, through sin, widened the gap between God (The Father) and man.

About Me

I come from an Indian Christian household, born and raised in India, where two things were of utmost importance: God and education. The priority of importance was given in that exact order, and nothing else mattered. My dad played a huge role in my life by keeping me on track because I was 'the middle child' and had a mind of my own.

I would do things because people challenged me, saying that I couldn't. And so I became a welding engineer. The typical Indian mentality is that girls do not need as much education as boys, but my dad was a visionary. He gave us freedom (within limits), provided for us, mentored us, and guided us in every step. He was the best preacher, a good father, and a generous giver. His sermons were effective – no one taught life application as well as he did. He was my hero.

I got married in December 2012 to a non-Indian. Although my parents were OK with it, others in our family and community gossiped, but I never cared much for the so-called society anyway. I was happy and content that God blessed me to be a wife, a mother (of three handsome, active boys), and an engineer. My husband and I were extremely grateful for how God blessed us and continues to bless us financially because of our careers.

There's more ...

It was March 2021, and as usual, I went about my busy day and did all the things I needed to do as a wife, mother, and employee. That night, I woke up from a dream that changed everything for me. I was sitting inside a prison cell praying with a man whose stature was much bigger than mine as he nodded in acceptance. The atmosphere was dull, grayish, pin-drop silent, with two other people sitting facing each other and hanging their heads down within the unlocked cell. I am not sure what I was praying about, but that wasn't the important part.

I woke up in disbelief, trying to understand what it meant for me to be in a prison cell. It was an uncomfortable situation and did not sit well with me. It bothered me so much that I was losing my peace over it, always irritated due to the unknown. I tried to ignore it, and the more I ignored it, the more it bounced back in my face. I told my husband about the dream, and he prayed for me.

One night after another typical day, I crocheted, then laid down and started praying. I asked God to show me what it all meant, what I had to do with a prison cell, and who was that man? I prayed for three months for an answer. During these three months, I had visions of many different things, including our family helping people in many ways. In pursuit of establishing some local contacts, my husband and I stumbled upon a gentleman, a drug addict for many years, who was now a pastor in Waco, TX. That night I prayed again.

During my prayer, I was convinced that God was calling us to Prison Ministry. It was vague at first; sometimes I still wonder about it. And when I prayed to know if God really wanted us to do this, He literally showed himself.

I saw a white chariot with seven white horses and a man clothed in white standing in the back, one foot set on a footstool. The chariot was in front of my eyes, not so close, but not far away. The clear night sky had no clouds, no disturbances of any sort. I could see that the man was mighty in his posture, command, and power. I felt like he could do anything, including commanding the horses with just a nod. Thus was his power; everything was in his control. The chariot slowly glided in front of my eyes. It was the most peaceful thing I had seen in a long time.

After this, I kept questioning the visions.

This cannot be true; I am tired.

I am just making things up in my head.

Why would God choose me?

God doesn't need me.

A couple of days later, I prayed for a second confirmation and saw the same chariot and the same man, followed by my deceased dad's face smiling. It was spine-chilling. I believed this vision was the confirmation that God had picked me (of all people) to do this job. God has a good sense of humour and threw in the last piece for extra surety. The whole experience was enlightening, profound, and soul-stirring. It was an eye-opener that God could give me intricate details and affirm what He wanted to accomplish through me. It was very, very humbling.

I shared this with my husband. I told him that I felt privileged to be called, and I wanted to be obedient to this calling, despite all odds. What followed were many conversations with God, and for every question, there was a perfectly crafted answer. Often, I thought, "Why does He even care to answer? As his clay, am I not supposed to do His will because he said so?" But God the Father does not work like an earthly parent. He loves us with a love that can win anyone and anything. He surely won my heart.

We formed Alpha – Omega, The Beginning and the End.

The sole purpose of this organization is to showcase the love of Christ by helping many incarcerated fellows and their families lead a normal and respectable life. Alpha – Omega is a place where people are not judged and can be appreciated as human beings with unique talents. The same God who cared to answer my question in detail cares about each and every person. Alpha – Omega, the Beginning and the End, seeks passionately to provide resources to all demographics to help break chains for the sake of future generations.

One day, we would like to provide food and shelter for the people released from their time in prison and teach them the skills they need to move on in the workforce and life. We desire to support them in transitioning from broken and imprisoned to a well-deserved second chance. And it can happen! It can happen because Jesus carried the shame, guilt, pain, and suffering on the cross – so you and I don't have to. And indeed! These people deserve a round of unconditional love.

I asked God, "Don't these people belong where they are? They committed a crime and a sin in your eyes, so why should they get a second chance?" The answer was clear as day. The response was, "You sinned too; did I not save you?" And he continued, "No sin is greater nor lesser." All creation is at the foot of the cross, falling short of His glory, waiting to be redeemed. There is no way to escape sin but by accepting Him, and there is no way of discarding his love.

When you accept Jesus as your saviour, He washes you in his blood that was dripping from the cross, not physically but spiritually. And so, as His creations, we want to bring forth this vision of turning lives to Jesus, making His name greater every day, resonating with His love, saving each soul, rescuing each spirit, and showing them what Jesus did.

We pray that our efforts will multiply as we show the way – Jesus's way. We hope to shine a small beacon of light deeply into people's lives, sow the seed of faith, and break the generational curse for families.

We will show them Heaven on Earth by giving them hope of a new creation in them, a new relationship with the Heavenly Father. Nothing can be more comforting than to know that the Father holds you in his hands. He promises a new Heaven on Earth for you if only you call upon His name and accept Him as your personal saviour.

Do we have all the years planned out for our mission? No!

We do not have a lot of details yet, including who to bring in as partners, but we have a vision. We pray that the right people, resources, and organizations come along our way, like-minded partners who share a similar vision and passion for Christ. We desire to partner with those who have become His laborers and seek Christ with their hearts. We seek those with a passion that resonates with God's love and a servant's heart that does not weigh earthly benefits.

I promised myself that I would not act upon anything that was not God-led. The ultimate purpose of Alpha – Omega is not to display my ideas but to show more of God's love.

When I asked God how exactly this was going to play out and what I must do, the answer I got was to trust and pray. So that's what I am going to do, and I also ask you all to pray alongside us, serve more fellows (and their families), make them great citizens for a new heaven and a new earth, and bring them one step closer to the Living God.

Join us in this unique and powerful way to serve God and His purpose. Your donations are appreciated, and your prayers go a long way. Open your hearts generously to assist the incarcerated.

The Grace of Lord Jesus be with God's people. Amen.

[Revelation 22:16].

ABOUT THE AUTHOR:
Ruth Sierra

D r. Ruth Sierra is a daughter, wife, mother to three hand-some boys, and an Engineer by profession. She has an established engineering career and has previously taught at two different universities.

Passionate for the word of God, Ruth has chosen to follow the path she's currently called to in obedience. Her passion has driven her to start a non–profit organization named Alpha – Omega, The Beginning and the End, along with a couple of local small businesses where she and her husband are dedicated to hiring people from incarcerated and homeless back-grounds only.

With many leadership skills, she passionately leads Alpha – Omega to effectively raise funds and distribute them in the most effective way to help and support the specified commu-nities.

Ruth's mission, along with her husband, is to proclaim the love of Christ to the people who most need it, break all gener-ational curses that are strongholds through prayer, and intro-duce them to the resurrection story, where all hope lies. They hope to create lifelong, passionate, mission-driven leaders and true laborers for Christ.

A life of freedom in Christ.

14

A World Where the Orphan Has a Home

Isaiah 117 House
Kaeley Moore for Sarah Beth Miller
Waco, Texas. United States.

Over five years ago, my husband and I became foster parents. Before then, everything I knew or heard about foster care was wrapped up in a negative stigma. I knew the horror stories of kids' bad behavior or foster parents opening their homes as a source of income. When our church highlighted foster care and adoption one spring, we heard a foster mom share her story. Her experience and heart were the perfect picture of God's heart for His children. It was the first time I saw foster and adoptive parents as the hands and feet of Christ. In that moment, I began to see foster care as brokenness turning into beauty and wholeness. Even with our brokenness, God adopts us all, gives us a place to rest, and provides for our needs. He makes us whole. This is foster care.

My husband and I always thought we would adopt, but we didn't know what it would look like or when it would happen. We didn't even talk about it until the car ride home from church that day. We were left thinking maybe foster care could be part of our story. It was a journey we didn't know to expect, but it was God ordained in a way that left us in awe.

We had so much love to give and an empty bedroom. There were kids who needed a home. Why would we not?! We had never been parents, though, and we were unsure of when we wanted to have biological children. So, we postponed foster care and spent the next year not discussing it. I tried to push it out of my mind, but I was always thinking about it. I researched foster care every day. I read articles and books, and eventually, the idea of fostering became something that I just couldn't set aside. After about a year, I found myself sobbing in the kitchen as I brought up the topic with my husband again. I told him I didn't have all the answers, but I truly felt we were supposed to do something. We made plans to attend the next state information session in our city. On that day, when we walked in, a placing agency was in attendance to share information about how they could help foster parents. A friend had recommended we look into this same agency. After the session, we sat in silence for a few minutes. I asked for my husband's thoughts. He said, "I knew we were doing this before we walked in the door." We both knew this was the right path for us. This was the moment I realized we had *each* felt a call that we knew needed our small "yes."

About nine months passed by the time we completed the application and orientation, in-person trauma-informed care and CPR training, online documenting and reporting trainings, home inspections, home study, and babysitting certification for our chosen babysitters. At that point, we were ready to be placed on the call list and begin accepting placements. Within the first few days, we received an email about a three-year-old little girl who needed a home. She needed a temporary place of transition where she could stay before reunifying with her family. At the time, her family was approved for 8-hour unsupervised visitation in a town on the other side of the state. We quickly realized this wasn't something we could do, and thankfully, our agency also realized this wasn't a good fit for us or the child. But still, it was hard to say no.

Within 48 hours after that decision, the phone began ringing as we settled in for bed. It was our agency-appointed caseworker with the news that we had the opportunity to love and care for another child. This time, we said "yes" to a sweet baby girl and a journey that would change our lives forever. As God would have it, we received the news of my pregnancy only five months later and finalized an adoption later that year.

As we planned and prepared for two children under 15 months old, we knew the right decision was to close our home and no longer accept foster care placements. But once you see it, you can't unsee it. Once you've seen the children, heard the needs, and shared your heart in this way, you can't forget about the needs in the community that your heart longs to help. Three years later, we were wading through a global pandemic with two little girls whose anthem is "wild as a mink, but sweet as soda pop." Our days were long and left me wondering where I would find myself next. I had been in a professional role at a local university for nearly six years, and although I truly enjoyed it, I felt there was more for me to do.

One night I stumbled upon a social media post for an organization called Isaiah 117 House that started very near my hometown in Tennessee. I quickly found myself scouring the internet to learn more. I read the details of the website and watched the videos I could find online. Immediately, I thought this was something our community needed. Based on our time in foster care, I knew there weren't a lot of resources in our community. Some local churches were doing their best, but there wasn't much structural support. There weren't enough organizations or official ministries that served in the foster care arena. Although I was interested, something held me back. Then God showed up a few months later through a Facebook post from an acquaintance of mine, Jennifer.

I knew Jennifer because she brought us a meal when we received our first placement three years prior. Come to find out, Jennifer had also become a foster parent and made connections with our local Child Protective Services (CPS) team. Her post shared that CPS needed cots and blankets because children without placements were sleeping on the floor in the conference room of their local office. This is one of the gaps that Isaiah 117 House aims to fill, so I jumped into action. Within 24 hours, I submitted a video and was asked to form a team. Jennifer was my first call. I was honored to have four women, including Jen, join me on this journey to bring an Isaiah 117 House to our community. We hoped to support children awaiting placement, CPS caseworkers, and foster families in a comprehensive way that our community had not seen before. We began raising awareness of this need and watched as God allowed us to witness a miracle in our community. We saw individuals of all ages rally around the mission, lives of strangers connect in ways only God can do, and love bind our community in a way that changed the future. We saw this happen because of our little "yes." It is incredible what God can do when we take the first small step of obedience.

The mission of Isaiah 117 House is to provide physical and emotional support in a safe and loving home for children awaiting foster care placement. We exist to reduce trauma for children on their removal day, to lighten the load for hardworking caseworkers, and to ease the transition for foster families. We do this by providing a comfortable, safe, and loving space for children and CPS caseworkers while they work to locate a long-term foster placement. Children of all ages are often left to wait in offices or conference rooms for hours and sometimes even overnight. These children are lonely, scared, without toys or comforts, and potentially in need of a bath and meal. We strive to remind each child, caseworker, and foster parent that they are loved and not alone.

As of August 2022, Isaiah 117 House has eleven open homes. Each home is staffed by volunteers who gave more than 11,000 hours of their time to over 1,300 guests who came through our doors in 2021. In partnership with child welfare departments, our organization provided resources for more than 400 individual children and nearly 200 foster families throughout the year. Our efforts continue to grow as we now have over 30 locations across six states, including many homes under construction. All because God is moving His people and building homes for children He has never forgotten. We pray that He will continue to rally a family of individuals and communities who feel called to defend the cause of the fatherless and that this mission will be one way the Church rises up across the country.

We will soon break ground at the Isaiah 117 House location in my own community, and I cannot wait to see this house become a reality for children in the foster care system and those who work diligently to support them. I know that the future is bright for Isaiah 117 House as God goes before us to guide the way, and I am so honored to be a part of the mission.

"Learn to do right; seek justice.
Defend the oppressed.
Take up the cause of the fatherless;
plead the case of the widow." -Isaiah 1:17

ABOUT THE AUTHOR
Sarah Beth Miller

I saiah 117 House provides physical and emotional support in a safe and loving home to children awaiting foster placement. The non-profit's goal is to reduce trauma for children on removal day, lighten the load for caseworkers, and ease the transition for foster families. Sarah Miller currently serves as the Texas State Director for Isaiah 117 House.

Connect with Isaiah 117 House:

15

A World Where Everyone Has a Helping Hand

Built on a Firm Foundation
Sara Gama
San Antonio, Texas. United States.

The Lord has given me a vision. I do not see how this will happen, but I trust God's plan. This will be a haven for anyone who needs help. Everyone has a hard time in life at some point, so why can't we reach out our hands and say, "You're not alone. Let me help you." Have you ever had that moment where someone would just reach out and say, "I've got you. Come with me."?

As a mompreneur myself, I love working with mothers and children. My joy is found when a lightbulb has gone off, and I can see their confidence increase as they discover that they have the tools to accomplish what they set their mind to. Come with me on this journey in my vision. Let me share with you what has been revealed to me. It is gorgeous and will help thousands of people. You, too, can be a part of this reality when it is up and going.

My husband and I are driving in our grey Dodge Ram onto a vast green, hundred-acre lot, greeted by cows. I can see open land all the way to where the sun meets the trees in the distance. With the windows down, the unmistakable smell of cow manure fills our noses. Just before the large tree line, there's a massive building, and as we get closer, we see it is a huge greenhouse. In this greenhouse, a large variety of vegetables, herbs, and fruits are growing. Beside the greenhouse is an area for chickens and goats to roam. They are providing us with their milk and eggs. The tree line is filled with rows of fruit trees. There is a large variety of apple, lemon, lime, and fig trees. On the opposite side of the road by the rows of trees is an enormous vineyard, growing all kinds of grapes. In a small area between all the trees is a small beehive. The bees provide the pollination of the trees and flowers galore, and they provide us with sweet honey. This place could feed an army if needed.

As we continue to drive down the rocky driveway, we can see a large blue building and several smaller buildings. The large building is surrounded by a large variety of beautifully scented and colorful flowers along the porch that enfolds the building. As we approach the large building, the wind sends us a scent of chlorine. The pool is in the building – a giant Olympic-sized pool. Just around the corner, we can see a game room complete with a pool table and table tennis being played by teenagers. Adults and young children are also using table hockey. The TVs have video game consoles, but at this moment, HGTV is playing. The game room has bright yellow paint over the walls.

Next door is a store, and this store is special. This yellow-green painted retailer is filled with donated toys, clothes, and miscellaneous knick-knacks, making this room feel more like home. Those coming in with nothing can shop here for whatever they need, free of charge.

Alongside the store is a giant sky-blue painted library filled with the undeniable smell of coffee. The library is filled with thousands of books and a beautiful sitting area. The sitting area here has beautiful pastel-colored chairs. The library has a computer lab for guests to research or fill out job applications. Classes will be held in this room for men and women to learn how to run their own home-based business created by the most trusted and successful leader I know, Martha Krejci. On the opposite end of this building is a gigantic teal-covered cafeteria with tables in rows. Oh, it smells wonderful. It radiates the smell of freshly cooked meals made with the food found on the land. Along the counter by all the utensils and napkins is a large beverage machine with a substantial variety of drinks. In the hallway sit some people alone while others are sitting in groups laughing hysterically. This sweet sound fills the halls.

Behind this building is a vast field that can be used for soccer or football. A tennis court is surrounded by a basketball court on one side and a volleyball court on the other. On the side of the volleyball court is the women and children's four- to five-floor dormitory. On the side of the basketball court is the men's four- to five-floor dormitory. Each dormitory has furniture, two bedrooms, and a full bath. There is a fully stocked kitchen on each main floor to cook when the cafeteria is closed.

Adjacent to the tennis court is another large building. This building has classrooms for children and adults. Jesus is taught here. Each classroom is filled with individual desks and school supplies for the children. There is a beautiful yellow music room filled with various instruments for anyone to learn how to make music. There are different trade schools for the adults who want to learn how to make clothes, work on cars, or learn carpentry. These trades will provide a job for them when they finish their courses and are ready to leave our facility. Just beside the school is a big playground for the children to play in.

For anyone wanting to work and make a small amount of money, jobs will be provided. They can choose between cooking in the cafeteria, being a housekeeper in the various buildings, or being a teacher in the school. The position of a janitor to clean the buildings will be available also. If there is an interest in taking care of the land, a landscaper and gardener position will be open. Everyone living on the campus will take rotations picking ripe provisions, learning about the land, and storing foods properly. Canning classes will be held as well. Everything we have to offer will be provided free of charge or at a small fee.

Further down the property is a big swimming hole with places to camp next to the water. There are several picnic tables and fire pits to make s'mores and prepare a meal. On the back end of the watering hole is a building that provides tents and chairs. There are also s'mores sticks and some firewood to build a fire. There are kayaks to paddle across the water.

This property will be for people from all walks of life that need help to get back on their feet. It is for the woman seeking shelter from the man beating her and her children. It is a place for those that got too deep into drugs and need help. It is a place for women who have left their abusive husbands and do not have a place to go. This property is for the sick and the widows, for the lost and lonely.

At the entrance of the property lies a sign: Built on a Firm Foundation. Here we can help men, women, and children get back on their feet. They will need to get a job on campus to reestablish their work-life and see their own potential, building up confidence. Every teenager and adult will be required to attend a class to learn how to manage their finances before they leave. They will learn how to grow their own food and harvest it. They will learn about the love of Jesus and the vision He has given me to help them. They will leave this property when their feet are back on the ground and ready to enter the world as a different person.

This vision of Built on a Firm Foundation will help thousands, and I can see it within my reach. My heart is overwhelmed with joy to envision those leaving with hope and having the tools they need to be successful after departing from us. I have no doubt that this will come to pass.

Can you see it? Can you smell the trees as the wind blows through them, sending their sweet scent for miles? Can you see children laughing for the first time in a long time because they finally feel safe? Do you see the woman who has feared for her life no longer hiding her face or dodging you because her confidence has been built with the love she has received? Can you see the man standing a few inches taller because he is free of the drugs that have plagued his life for far too many years? Do you see him building his confidence through developing his skill in automotive care? He will be able to leave here and get a job to provide for himself for the first time in a long time. Do you see the children's eyes light up as they pick their food from the ground? Do you see the impact of learning to reap what they planted? Oh, what joy it brings!

Matthew 7:24-26 says: "Therefore everyone who hears these words of Mine and does them will be like a wise man who built his house on the rock. And the rain fell, and the floods came, and the winds blew and beat against that house; and yet it did not fall, for its foundation had been built on the rock. Everyone who hears these words of Mine and does not act on them will be like a foolish man who built his house on the sand." The verse discusses building your life on the sand or the rock. If you build your house on the rock, you will not float away. Your house isn't your physical home; this is about your life. If your life is built on a firm foundation (Jesus Christ), your life won't float away. Christ calls us to pick up our cross but never promises the weight to be light. We all go through difficult times, and no one is exempt from the pain of walking this path.

May this happen on Earth as it is in Heaven. Will you join me in prayer for this vision to come to pass? Will you join me in trusting God to provide what we need to be successful for this vision to come to pass? Will you love on people that are hurting? Will I see you here one day lending a hand?

ABOUT THE AUTHOR:
Sara Gama

S ara Gama is a mother to four beautiful children. She has over nine years of experience educating preschool and elementary-age children. Her experience includes teaching in both preschool and Sunday school environments. She also teaches her own children at home. Sara has many creations on Amazon that can be found by looking up her name. What she loves most is working with mothers, helping them educate their children and become more confident in their abilities as parents. When she's not busy being a mom or a teacher, she enjoys reading, hiking, and spending time with her family.

Connect with Sara:

16

A World Where Anyone Knocked Down by Life Remembers How to Dream Again

Kat Hall

Pass Christian, Mississippi. United States.

God truly has given us all a slice of Heaven on Earth if we take the time to find and embrace it. He has blessed us with many treasures that will light up and lighten the loads of our hearts and souls if we would only take out the daily dose of trash that the world continually drops onto us. We must take the time to focus on the blessings that continually surround us. His light and love are everywhere because they are within each of us.

Seeing my spouse crumble in front of me as a result of a traumatic brain injury (TBI) has been the most excruciating experience I have ever had to go through. The man I love and have devoted my life to has gone through things that I would never wish for anyone, and I choose to stay by his side to love and cherish him forever. Not one day goes by that I do not feel a deep desire to love him the best I can in each moment we have together. No matter how hard life gets, how difficult a situation may become, and no matter what the unknown holds for our family, I choose him every day. Again and again. Forever and ever.

As I lay in the bed next to him and just watch him take deep breaths of God-given air, I am thankful for this journey we have taken. I have grown to love him to depths I did not know existed. I did not know that I would be able to love someone more than the face-value type of love that so many people experience.

At the beginning of our marriage, we had a short time to build our dreams together before my husband had his accident. We saw his goals begin to come to fruition and then suddenly get torn away from him. Those who survive a TBI understand this type of grief and loss, and they know the depths of despair experienced by a person and their family when these accidents happen.

My husband's brain injury occurred during his active-duty military service. So many people have gotten hurt in service and lost the dream of making the military their career. This experience has been a nightmare that we have had to love each other through. My husband had the dream to complete his military career, retire, and move on to civilian life with a second career. His accident changed our life trajectory and threw us on a new path in one blink of an eye.

We were met with many unknowns in the years following his accident. During the waiting period, his military orders got put on hold. We didn't know how soon the Navy medical board would process his accident and eventual medical retirement. We didn't know how we would take care of our family or where we would go. These thoughts and questions went through my head repeatedly.

Becoming an advocate was not an easy task. The Veteran's health care system has many loops I had to go through just to be able to speak for my husband when he couldn't speak for himself. His TBI put him in a fight or flight mode when seeing doctors. He would shut down, and sometimes he could not fully communicate what he was going through, so I had to step in. Over the years, and with many new health issues arising, the changes have been difficult to handle. His neuro-fatigue has increased to the point that if he exerts himself in any activity, he gets exhausted, and all he can do is sleep or rest. Since his brain can no longer regulate his body temperature, he can't be out in the heat. When his brain gets exhausted, it gets worse.

I share this because, as a couple, we have seen and experienced things that can take us to a dark place. This dark place wants to hold onto us and not let us go. What has kept us out of this dark place is how God has shown us His Heaven on Earth, His type of love. We can elect to stay in the dark place or focus on our blessings from God. I had to reach a point where I *decided* to find the blessings in my day – each and every day. Now I choose to see the blessings in each situation we go through, embrace the light and love that surrounds us, and see Heaven on Earth in my daily life.

With as much stuff as I've gone through in my own life, I always try to find the daily blessings God puts before me. In the hardest of moments, God will show you the simple blessings in life. Those blessings will touch your heart and even melt your soul so deep inside that you will cherish them forever. Life is so challenging sometimes that I can only take one step at a time. But I know that God has my tomorrow, even when I can't focus to take care of my today. Having the courage to hold onto my faith and having hope in the Lord has strengthened me. It can support you, too.

I don't know where I'd be today if it weren't for my faith. I don't know if I would be able to push through if I didn't have God on my side. So many people don't believe in the Creator, God, or something bigger than themselves. I don't understand how God can do things and allow things to happen when he can just fix them instantly. But knowing where we were and where we are today, I can see that God has supported us as we moved forward with courage in our journey of faith.

Today, I have been reflecting on what these past few years have brought us. This experience has brought our little family closer together in different ways. While the kids were away at college, we were physically apart, but we have worked our way back together, and all the kids have recently moved back home.

We have blossomed in dreaming and believing in what can happen in our lives, what we can do for our family, and what God has in store for us all. We have experienced joy in reflection and have seen the potential in many areas of life.

Don't get me wrong; we've been through A LOT. We've seen so many changes and some hard, crazy, heartbreaking things. We've gained some things; lost some things. We were empty nesters until Covid brought one of our three kids home. We became grandparents and so much more. Overall, we've shared SO MUCH LOVE. A lot of God's Divine Blessings have happened and continue to happen.

We have discovered what's important: family, growth, and blessings.

So, as you reflect on your family's years and the things you've gone through, choose to grow through the hard things by focusing on God's blessings in your life. Sometimes we don't see them when we hurt or are deep in the moment, but the blessings surround us daily.

Seek, and you shall find the blessings. Sometimes they are right under your nose; sometimes they are new thoughts or perspectives, but blessings are there. Once you find them, truly embrace them. Think about how they have changed and moved you in life and how you can use what you have learned to serve others. Blessings are the testimonies in our lives. They are always worth sharing and can inspire, encourage, bless, and give hope to others. When our growth in life takes us to new levels and heights, reflection helps us know what has helped us, what has hindered us, what works, and what doesn't. Reflect on how you can do things better or use what works to continue down your life's path towards what God has in store for you. Thank God for blessings. YOU, my friend, are a blessing in my life. I thank God for YOU.

Isaiah 45:1-13

Today as I sit and read this passage of scripture, my heart is drawn to who I am in this life, how God has shaped me through my experiences, and the life choices I have made with the will He has given me. I did not choose some of the things that have fallen into my lap; however, they have prepared me to manage the things that I need to tend to so that it is pleasing to Him.

Isaiah 45 shows me that I am a caregiver by God's handiwork, and God is with me through this 100%. Verse 2 says, "I will GO before you and level the uneven places; I will shatter the bronze doors and cut the iron bars in two."

From this scripture, my mind vividly brings me to pushing my love in his wheelchair. We all know that a wheelchair cannot easily roll on a gravel path. The rocks make it get stuck, twist up the front wheels, and cause anguish and frustration. When walking on paths, as I did just yesterday, I find myself kicking rocks off the sidewalks. I clear the way to prevent hang-ups for my fellow people in any wheeled capacity and to assist with a smooth journey down the path.

God will be the most gracious one who opens the door for us, and he will show me those who give of themselves to help me along my path. When a person takes two seconds out of their day to hold the door for us, I know that is God showing me that he not only shattered that door wide open, but He is sending his angel to bless me. As the door opens, it feels like a parent with open arms inviting a child for a warm embrace.

Oh, how God is moving through me in this one vivid picture, making me think of my parents. God gave them their loving, open arms and the sweet smell of their essence. I love the feeling of their hair along my cheek as I bury my face into their neck to smell them deeply. You know we all do it. We love someone so dearly that we just want to 'suck in' all we can at that moment. To hold onto and cherish and relish that second in their warm embrace. Just pause a moment and stay right here. Breathe it in. Wrap your arms around your own shoulders right now and feel that embrace. Let the embrace take you to that special place of love, warmth, comfort, safety, and home.

For some of you, this is a hard place to find, as you may have had a hard upbringing or childhood, or there is no memory there. Picture this from your closest friend, spouse, or loved one. When was the last time you received such a warm embrace that you just wanted to stay longer? How did it feel and smell? Where were you? Take yourself back to that place. Hold onto this feeling and wrap your arms around your own shoulders. Feel your hands upon your shoulders as if you are in that cherished embrace with your person. Breathe it in, and let the embrace take you to that special place of love, warmth, comfort, safety, and home.

These feelings of comfort, safety, and home are what God wants us to feel. Have you experienced that kind of feeling? I have with my relationship with my husband. Unconditional love is the love that God wants us to feel. I have felt this with my parents. No other love can compare to how He wants us to feel. He wants us to feel it physically, like the warm hug from your husband, a cool breeze on a hot day, your favorite comfortable, cozy sweater, or the feeling of a baby's soft skin on your cheek. He wants us to feel it emotionally through true joy and bliss in His blessings. He wants us to experience it visually through the beautiful blessings he puts in our path along our life journey. He wants us to experience being creators like Him. He wants us to feel it spiritually as He guides us through life's turmoil to the testimonies of his compassion and love.

These are all examples of what Heaven on Earth is to me. Let's see what Your Heaven on Earth can do in your life. How can it help you through a tough time or turn your perspective around? How can it make your life better or bless you and your family? You can learn to embrace it too. I am here to support you.

ABOUT THE AUTHOR:
Kat M. Hall

K at M. Hall is a family-focused, faith-filled wife, mom, and Gigi. She is a Military Caregiver to her different-ly-abled Veteran hubby, Jon. She is passionate about empow-ering and inspiring other families while they are juggling care-giving and raising active families. As a Certified OOLA Life Coach, she links arms and helps others transform their lives from the unknowns and chaos to a balanced and abundant life. She helps others through finding their Faith, Discovering Hope, and Sharing Love. Building their family's love legacy and blessing others is what she's all about.

Connect with Kat:

Acknowledgments

The book that you're holding in your hands is the culmination of many incredible people's love, time, gifting, hard work, and emotional energy, without whom its existence would not have been possible.

I am so thankful to my husband and best friend, Danny, who seems to believe in my crazy ideas so much that he creates and protects the time, space, and resources needed to get them across the finish line.

To Heather Haurbaugh, who protected and cared for this idea in its embryonic stages, especially when it needed protection from my own doubts and fears. Heather, your friendship and cheerleading have gotten me through every phase of this project with just a little more courage each time.

To Meggan Larson, whose experienced and wise guidance saved me from my own ambitious naivety more than once, and whose friendship is a treasure.

To Lydia Eppic, Belinda Mclean & Mary DeAcetis, who generously shared their expertise and work with each of the authors at different stages of this project, enriching their experience and the finished product you hold in your hands.

To my mother & father-in-love, Laurinda & Carlos, whose presence made the many finishing touches this project needed fun and easy.

To our editorial team; Kelley Stone, Christianna Johnson, Sharlene Mohlman, Kaeley Moore, Erika Harston Noll, and Hannah Mwenda. Thank you for all of your hard work and patience as you facilitated the sharing of the stories that honours both the readers and our authors.

To the authors, the ladies who volunteered to pour their most vulnerable experiences into these pages. They raised their hands to bear witness to one another and, more importantly, to themselves in the hopes that you will discover the courage to do the same for others and yourselves. It takes great courage to tell your story publicly, even more so to subject it to the scrutiny of editors, proofreaders, and the public. Be gentle with their courage.

Finally, to the friends, families, children, and spouses connected to every person who had a hand in bringing this project to life.

Here's to the brave, kind, and curious women in our world. I hope that as you bear witness to the stories in this book, you'll come to bear witness to your own. You are brave, you belong, and your dreams matter.

Lauren. xx

OTHER BOOKS IN THE ART OF FLOURISHING SERIES
AVAILABLE ON AMAZON

AVAILABLE ON:
SPOTIFY, APPLE PODCASTS,
OVERCAST, IHEART RADIO & MORE

LOOKING FOR YOUR PEOPLE?

THE FLOURISH HUB IS A VIRTUAL
SUPPORT NETWORK & GATHERING
PLACE FOR WOMEN & MOTHERS IN
ENTREPRENEURSHIP

THE-FLOURISH-HUB.MN.CO

Also By Flourish Hub Media Company

The Heart-Centered Woman's Guide to Healthy Boundaries.
By Lauren da Silva
Courage, Dear Heart: An Anthology. Curated by Lauren da
Silva
On Being & Belonging: An Anthology. Curated by Lauren da
Silva

About the Curator

Lauren da Silva

Lauren da Silva is a champion for curiosity, connection, and creativity. She is also a 'safe-space creator' and is known for creating cathartic and soul-nourishing online and in-person environments where women can show up as themselves, share their stories, and support one another in the process.

Lauren is the bestselling author of *The Heart-Centered Woman's Guide to Healthy Boundaries*, the host of "The Art of Flourishing" podcast, and co-host of The Flourish Hub virtual mutual-support community for solo-mompreneurs. She also co-hosts an annual retreat in Cocoa Beach, FL, and Flourish Week, an annual hybrid gathering in her new hometown of Waco, Tx.

When she is not reading, writing, teaching, or connecting, you can find her painting, wandering around in the woods, or in her backyard, tending to her butterfly garden with her children and her small flock of backyard chickens. :)

Connect with Lauren:

Made in the USA
Monee, IL
23 December 2022